# Windows Fan, Linux Fan

A true story about a spiritual battle between a Windows
fan and a Linux fan!

Fore June

# Windows Fan, Linux Fan

## A true story about a spiritual battle between a Windows fan and a Linux fan!

Copyright @ 2003 by Fore June

CreateSpace, a DBA of On-Demand Publishing, LLC.

ISBN: 1-453-81768-9

# Contents

# About the Author

Fore June is an independent Internet Service Provider (ISP) who provides various kinds of Internet services to the public. He founded or co-founded a few Internet service companies; the web site of one of them won the PC Magazine award.

Fore holds a B.Sc. degree in Physics.

# Chapter 1    Introduction

The growth of a technology company is like a living thing and like all life it must wax and wane, adapt itself and undergo trials and transformations. The glory of computer companies is no exception to this rule. It is unstable and liable to change, gorgeous one moment, gone the next, sometimes as real and close as a cup of coffee carried in hand, sometimes as unreal and remote as the moon shadow in water. And in time when one company appears to be dominative and undefeatable, a completely new type of technology more and more often emerges and makes business difficult for it. At first it was the Mainframe of Big Blue that conquered the whole computing world. Unable to fend off the onslaught of Minicomputers, its glory diminished and faded in the 1980s when the growth of Mini manufacturers like Wang and DEC was exploding like supernova stars and attracting focus and admiration of the whole world. But the Mini brightness was also like supernovas, short-lived and transient. Not adapted fast enough to face the UNIX challenge, both Wang and DEC went out of business before last century ended. The early 1990s were the golden age of UNIX, which dominated enterprise computing. The UNIX vendors seemed to own the world and began to polarize the UNIX OS in the name of creating innovative features. There were hundreds of UNIX versions around, each of which differed slightly from others. UNIX companies thought they could partition the computing world but in reality their glory was also governed by the rule of life.

While UNIX vendors were busy fighting each other, another operating system (OS) quietly emerged in the market with the will to dominate all computing systems. The OS was named Windows NT where NT stands for "new technology". At first, nobody took notice. The critics said that NT was just a rehash of existing technologies. They believed that it was a niche product introduced by a company, which stole ideas from others and was an intellectual thief – the lowest of the low. But soon the critics were proved wrong, dead wrong. By 1996, Windows NT became the Goliath of the computing world.

In that year, Windows NT reached the high point of its glory, which unfolded in wide acceptance in the public and in finding its way in almost all small to medium organizations. Hardly a day had passed by without the news of an organization switching from UNIX to NT. The war of OS ended in the year. Victory was declared and Windows Empire became the king of kings. Since then one empire ruled all and no one dared to challenge it and no one would, not even the government, for anyone who had challenged it had been crushed and had sunk into the abyss of darkness. For the first time in computing history, the rise of the Windows Empire seemed to defy the rule of life.

While the Empire was trumpeting the glory and superiority of its OS, many computing professionals felt sad and lost about the end of the OS war. They grew sad because they had expected a unified OS and the gradual extinction of confusing versions to bring a brightening of technology and easing of human life, to advance humans a step closer to the brave new world, but now a mono OS seemed to have betrayed and deceived them inasmuch as it had brought them nothing but evil monopoly, power abuse, standards polarization, security breaching, illegal business tactics, and world wide virus threats. They found their published work stolen, their innovations misused. Less and less could a software company innovate and grow with dignity. Less and less could a standards institution stand up against the Empire to operate independently. The destiny of computing seemed to be controlled by one empire. The reality had been particularly unfriendly to the academics. Distinguished alumni were dumped and fouled; college dropouts spoke loud. Cheaters got rich; pioneers died broke. Humans fought for thousands of years to get rid of the imperial system, to abolish the rule of kings only to find that they were again ruled by a camouflaged new kingdom wrapped with fake arguments.

At the moment when pioneers ceased to innovate, when thinkers felt hopeless, when engineers filled with despair, when programmers faced the dilemma of choosing between slavery with wealth and freedom with hardship, a quiet movement, like a dim star traveling across the infinite dark sky, suddenly appeared from nowhere. A loosely coupled constellation called "open source community" was established by a group of compassionate computing professionals over the world. They advocated a very strange idea, which would shock anyone who first heard about it. They gave away their work for free. They asked you to disclose your codes to the world, to share your ideas, and to give in order to receive. Computer codes should be shared freely instead of sold as property, they insisted. Though the open-source concept was reliable, proclaiming order, promising duration, and renewing hope, the star was so dim, high and remote that hardly anyone outside the computing society would notice its existence and understand its philosophy. Seemingly so aloof and far and opposed to business concepts on earth, so hated by Windows Empire, the open source movement was long laughed at as child play. Slowly and lonely, the dim star moved across the dark sky along a fixed path. In the early 1990s, the community introduced an OS called Linux to the mass, the kernel of which was derived from MINIX, a reduced and simplified version of UNIX developed by a Professor of Computer Science in Netherland. However, the OS was not developed by any single individual or by any single organization. It was the joint product of the efforts of tens of thousands of volunteer programmers and the dream of many souls around the world. It was free, open, and reliable. Anybody could download the OS free. Anybody could reproduce the OS without paying any royalties. It was a legend. It was hard to believe yet it was true. More and more computing professionals woke up and began to love and embrace it. But I was not one of them.

Rather, I began to study Windows NT in the early 1990s. Windows NT was extensible, portable, reliable, and scalable. It was designed for international use with source-level compatibility to applications that follow the POSIX specifications, the standard of UNIX. I liked NT because its design philosophy fits my lazy taste. In a UNIX system, you had to remember the exact command and its exact parameters. If you did not use the commands often, you would soon forget their exact names. Here an NT system required no more memorization of commands. Everything was point-and-click. At each step, the graphical user interface (GUI) reminded you what you needed to do next. There were no more complex jargons and no more mysteries. Administration of computer systems became painless and joyful. It was almost like a dream came true. The more I played with it, the more I liked it. I told everyone to take note – NT would reshape the course of computing; it was an OS well worth studying. I called it the *OS of the Century*. I was so enthusiastic and passionate about Windows NT that I was known to some of my friends as *Windows Fan*. ( Image below: An IBM 704 mainframe of 1956 )

# Chapter 2 The Fisherman

In 1996, the year the OS war ended, the Internet age began to dawn. The Web emerged and was about to explode. In America, the economy was booming. High tech share prices were rising like rockets at Cape Canaveral. But outside America, life seemed difficult. Japan was in recession. Russia was in chaos. Europe was in decline and the Asian Financial Storm was on the way to ruin the region. Just when a large portion of the world was ravaged with the plague, the Internet brought new hope. Some believed the IT industry was sufficient to heal the afflicted. At first only the computer professionals and a handful of people knew about it. Then the rumors of it rapidly spread to everywhere, like a fire sweeping through a grass plain, catching everyone by surprise and unprepared. While everyone spoke about it, many believed it and many doubted it. Many, however, immediately went on their way to start their dot-com. Many splendid and incredible things were reported about the Internet. Many found new lives and many made big fortunes. Teenagers became millionaires. Millionaires became billionaires. All these happened overnight. The doubters, however, criticized that the dot-coms were an illusion, and were bubbles that would do the economy more harm than good. They shunned all high tech companies in their investment portfolio.

Nevertheless, the rumors about Internet sounded sweet. The reports were redolent with magic. The world was sick. Life was suffering and here there seemed bright future, here there seemed to be an economy consuming no energy, an industry producing no pollution, joyful, clean, full of noble promises, full of hope. Everywhere there were rumors about dot-coms. Everywhere there were reports about their magic. Intellectuals, young and old, all over the world took notice, feeling a temptation and a longing.

I too heard and read the rumors from friends, relatives, newspapers, magazines and many weird sources. Each piece of news was heavy with hope, heavy with doubt. Wherever miraculous stories of the Internet rang out, I felt yearning, felt excitement.

For a long time, I had avoided trading real estates and speculating on stocks because I wanted to create and produce instead of living off by selling and buying. Being a science teacher, I had lived a world with peace and quietness and spent all my effort in teaching. If people were so interested in money, that's their business. I had my own reality and destiny. Year after year, my friends and acquaintance had told me that working in education was a dead end, a career that would bring neither fame nor wealth. They might be laughing at me but I absorbed all the laughter as a tree absorbs rain. That was my world perception and reality until I heard about the Internet rumors.

*Teaching is a holy task. It deserves one to dedicate wholly to the task.* I told myself. But when the intimate connection with the students began to fade over years, when the compassion in teaching began to diminish with repetitive work, when the lack of money forced me to reside in an area with the nation's worst air quality, the world's reality began to bully and change me. Slowly and hesitantly, greed and fear crept into my soul. Slowly, like the sand of a desert entering a beautiful vegetation land, slowly filling and eroding it, so did the reality and inertia crept into my soul; it slowly filled the soul, made it heavy, made it greedy.

Buddha had taught us that the mind is the root of everything. Now the thought of getting rich had crept into my mind and I was aware of a strong yearning of the Internet mounting within me. One day, the yearning had become intense. "Where," I asked myself, "where does it come from? What is the reason for feeling the yearning of the Internet? Does it arise from greed or passion? Or from fear of falling behind? Or because I want to do something significant? Not many of us live to our full potential. We linger in the lowland because we are afraid to climb the mountains which steepness and ruggedness have dismayed us. The world has laughed at me. I want to fight back, to start a business, to get rich. No, not any more. I had gone through battles to get my degrees; I had fought my wars to get my tenure and promotions. I have enough and I want to relax and retire."

There were two voices luring me in opposite directions, one voice telling me to seize the opportunity to start a business on Internet to get rich, and the other voice telling me to relax and enjoy life. I felt torn between these two voices. To release the mounting pressure of the yearning, I took Sherily, my three-year old daughter outside to have a walk in a warm and sunny day. However, the thoughts of getting rich hovered in my mind. A mixture of feeling of greed, fear, compassion and jealousy came over me like an itchy sensation and gradually it was turning into a tornado, which tended to torment me. I was deep in memory and the things around me seemed to vanish. An image suddenly flashed in my mind.

For a moment, I was a twelve-year old again, chasing with my brother Evans and other kids in the crackling autumn grass on a large dried rice field. Under one of the shade trees, Uncle Seven was sitting bolt upright and staring at us. Uncle Seven was a middle-aged man with a dignified but stern and rigid face. He had evidently been looking at us for some time. His eyes were keen and hard, but with intimate expression, like the eyes of a man, who is used to observe the world full with curiosity and intimacy or sympathy, who likes to bring warmth and happiness to people. He slowly stood up and gazed at us with a warm smile. He was holding in his hand an electric car with a little flashing red light. We had never seen anything this cool before. "Look. There are three trees at the opposite side of the stream, " he said, pointing to his right with the little car. "Lets have a race. Whoever first touches the middle tree is the winner and he will own this car. Remember, the middle tree is your destination." I followed his gaze. Uncle Seven was testing our will and endurance. The trees were far away. We had to run through the dried field, stumble over the mud and cross the stream. But the prize was well worth the effort. Our eyes widened with excitement and immediately positioned for the race. "One, two, three. Go!" Uncle Seven yelled. Though I was twelve years old, I already had the intuition that the shortest distance between two points is a straight line. The middle tree. That was my goal, my target. I headed straight towards it. But Evans seemed not to pay attention to what Uncle Seven had said. He ran towards the right tree. He was the only kid who made this mistake. "The middle one, Evans," I yelled. He seemed not to hear what I said. *Dummy, you are on the wrong path. You never pay attention to anything. You are always a dreamer and never do anything right!* The distraction slowed me down and I was slightly behind other kids. I was upset and angry with Evans. *Shame on you!* I felt frustrated and slowed down to a walking. "Don't give up, Fore!" Uncle Seven was jogging past me and tried to cheer me up. I turned my walk into a depressed half-hearted run. When I reached the destination, everyone was there already. I asked impatiently, "Who won?" Every kid looked at Evans. I was puzzled.

"That was impossible! He was on the wrong path and ran a longer distance!"

"Yes, Evans was the first kid who touched the middle tree," Uncle Seven said, handing the electric car to Evans.

I was totally absorbed in my own reflection. Suddenly, I heard my daughter utter a cry. Her cry brought me back to the real world and I immediately found that she slipped and hurt her hand. I was profoundly frightened. I blamed myself for not watching her carefully. Her cry woke me up. *Wealth was transitory. Fame was an illusion.* I made up my mind: *Get rid of the idea of starting a business; shut your-self off from the rumors of the Internet; take good care of your family.*

In an instant, all the thoughts about Internet became dormant and re-treated to reside deep in my mind. As all this happened, I suddenly felt emotionally relieved and realized the profound value of life.

As flowers bloomed and withered, spring went and summer came. My dream of starting a business on Internet had gradually faded and become hazy. I no longer desired to work on the Internet, which had been evolving rapidly. I no longer thought about the dot-com rumors. Instead, I took Sherily to all kind of child theme parks. There she experienced the wonders in Sea World. There she explored the fantasies and adventures in Disneyland. I saw her grow happily. One day I took her to Big Bear Lake, which was hidden deep in large mountains about a hundred miles east of Los Angeles. On our way to the lake, I drove along Freeway 60, passing through Riverside and San Bernardino counties, the two areas that had the worst air quality in the country. The smog was so heavy that my eyes were irritated and tears dropped. We could not see beyond a couple miles. Unable to resist the destructive forces of economics, the blue sky was vanishing. No wonder that the regions had the highest lung cancer rate in the nation.

I drove without any break and unconsciously I turned into Highway 18, which spiraled up the mountains. After another half hour driving, the blue sky began to emerge again. The blue sky cast a friendly look at the brightly shining mountains. The blossoms of some unknown plants flickered and waved between tiny trees. Everything was comfortable and enchanting. When I tore my eyes from the beloved landscape to look downward, I saw a cloud of darkness without the light of the day. It was a multi-layer dark cloud; a dark yellowish layer was sandwiched between two dark gray layers, like the clay in a fishing pond, dark and heavy. Nothing could be seen beyond the layer, though tens of thousands of people were residing below it. I did not know exactly what the layer was composed of. But one thing was sure: it was poisonous. What could we do? Most of us would rather breathe poisonous air than build and use electric trains to commute. Buddha had long recognized that life is suffering. Human suffers destiny just as wood suffers water and water suffers earth. In the name of building a brave new world, we suffered this poisonous air. We had to keep enduring this ugly environment. That's our fate. Strange was this fate. Round and round, I made numerous turns and the road seemed never end. After I had driven for a long time, we finally reached Big Bear Lake and I parked on a hillside. When Sherily and I got out of the car, we were astonished by the environment. The place was pristine, like a time machine to a period before humans were on the planet. Stunned by its crystalline waters, delicate rocks, and distilled clean air, we slowly walked along the lakeshore, through the evergreen pines, which were old beyond guessing. There was green and blue, sky and lake, woods and mountains, all beautiful, all mysterious and enchanting. Each breath and each step were like a sail on the lake, beneath the sail of a ship full of treasures, full of joy. Sherily walked on slowly, quietly absorbed in the natural wonders. Gradually, we walked deep into the woods, far away from the parking place. I had loved forests ever since I was a kid and this one seemed to me especially beautiful. While I was watching a squirrel climbing a large pine tree, I noticed a track leading through a thicket of high ferns, which rose like a miniature forest within the great forest. It was a narrow winding footpath. We cautiously pressed between the ferns and followed where it led. After a while we came upon a huge rock extending from the shore into the lake. We climbed and scrambled up the rock. When we reached the top, we were amazed to find a tree growing out of the rock, a sturdy tree with some strong branches and thick leaves. There it stood, beautiful and odd, hard and stiff in the rock. And beneath the tree sat an old man with both hands gripping a fishing rod.

Still and straight, the old man sat motionless but sang and whistled softly. Hanging on the rugged rock was a small fishing basket, which dipped into water on his right side. On his left side lay a tiny basket, which could be opened and contained some fishing baits. In the breeze of the blue lake, Sherily and I sat quietly and watched the old man fishing. I listened to the tune of his songs, slightly moved; it had been once familiar to me. It was the melody of one of the well-known Russian folk songs. The whistling was wonderfully sweet, with soft and pleasing notes, unusually pure, as happy and as natural as the songs of bird.

I sat and listened, enchanted and at the same time filled with curiosity. The old man seemed to be an unaffected person, and had something so pleasing that even a shy stranger dared speak to him. I signaled Sherily not to disturb the old man. He saw us sitting and listening, just for a moment then smiled at us with understanding as he continued his fishing and singing. His glance cheered me.

We sat patiently on the rock to watch him fish. The lake was quiet. I gazed into the water where fishes glided in the dark greenish blueness. Flickering patches appeared here and there in the still, glittering surface of the lake. The small fishes, swimming and gliding in groups wandered around. They swarmed in circles. Suddenly like wafting snowflakes, they rushed away and down, hundreds upon hundreds, in mysterious smooth motion, vanishing beyond the deep blue lake. Then another swarm of fish came from nowhere and swarmed towards the surface of the lake. Despite the amazingly coordinated movement, scientific studies had shown that there was no leader among the fishes. Their behavior was purely collective. Without any leader, it seemed that they were happy and free, enjoying every moment of the wonderful life and were unaware of any food bait. Their fluttery movement did not make any ripple in the lake. No one paid any attention to the bait either because they were not aware of its existence or because they enjoyed swimming and playing more. While watching their mysterious fish movement, I suddenly noticed that a long time seemed to have passed as the sun was setting. The old man still failed to catch any single fish. At the moment I wanted to get up and leave the rock, the old man stopped singing and whistling. There was silence. Then I saw a smile appearing in his face. Suddenly, he popped the rod with both hands. A small fish shot into the air, flapping its tail fiercely. With his right hand still gripping the rod, his left hand picked up and opened the basket to catch the falling fish, and unhooked it before pouring it into the basket that was dipping in the water. New bait was hooked and dipped into water. The whole action was in one coherent move, effortless and youthful. His body, from head to toe, from left to right was not acting as separating parts but as a whole with economical motions and quiet agility; it looked like an orient martial art movement, governed by strict rules which had been practiced a thousand times and brought to a tranquil dexterity.

Now the whole fishing game rebooted anew as he sang and whistled as before. This time, it did not take him long to repeat the same sequence of motion as another larger fish was caught. "The old man has super skill in fishing," I talked softly to myself and was enthralled by his sublime movement.

After he had gone through the process a dozen times, I was unable to further suppress my excitement. I raised my voice to speak to the old man, "I wish I could fish like you." He smiled and nodded but did not say anything.

Even while I was still enthralled by his sublime movement, which I had watched for so long and which looked so persuasively meaningful, a strange thought gripped me. I did not know exactly what the thought was. Then suddenly I knew. The fishes should have long filled the basket. How could such a small basket hold so many fishes, some of which were as long as one foot? With puzzle in my eyes, I gazed and gazed at the basket. Then the old man noticed my puzzled gaze. With a smiling face, he slowly pulled the basket from water. Something unbelievable appeared. There was no fish in the basket! Looking more carefully, I finally recognized that the basket had no bottom cover. It was simply a pipe allowing a fish to go back to the lake smoothly. With a mixture of curiosity and awe, I said, "Fisherman, it seemed that a big fish had destroyed your basket bottom and let all fishes escape."

"My basket has been like this for years. What's your name?" said the old man with a warm smile.

"I am Fore. Are you fishing?" I said.

"Yes, certainly, as you can see," said the old man, glaring at us with another warm smile.

"No, I can't see. Where are your fishes?"

"I come here for fishing, not for fishes."

"What do you mean? You catch a fish and put it back to the lake. You call this fishing?" "I enjoy the process of fishing. I am joyful whether I catch any fish or not. I am glad that I am here. So now do you still wish to fish like me?"

I hesitated, uncertain what to say, how many of my thoughts I ought to reveal. I was silent, deep in thought. I had too many wishes. I wish this and wish that and at the end I wish the world be perfect. But the world itself, being in and around us has never been perfect and will never be. Finally, I said firmly, "No. Now I only have one wish. I wish I would not have any more wishes. I am glad that I am here and I am glad that I meet you."

The sun was almost set. We said good-bye to the old man.

When Sherily and I got home, I felt that something had left me, like the cocoon a caterpillar sheds. The Internet dream began returning. It was different from before, gentler and softer, but just as appealing and alluring, just as desirable and glimmering as it had been. I convinced myself I should participate in the new economy. This was a path worth seeking though no one would show the path and no one knew exactly where it would end. I decided to start a business on the Internet. It was not wealth and fame, nor power and amusement that prompted me to make the decision. What I wanted most of all was to participate in the adventures of Internet and to experience something remarkable and unusual of the real world. I had one single goal: to become an Internet Service Provider (ISP), to connect users to the Internet, and to provide Internet services to the public.

Big Bear Mountain

Big Bear Lake

# Chapter 3    Life of an ISP

For days, I had been searching the Web for the adoption of Linux in a business. It's not that I was crazy about Linux. It's not that I was even like Linux. If I had sufficient capital, I would have used all Windows machine in my business, but I only had saved about $12,000. I'd finally come to the conclusion that I need to use both Linux and Windows.

My knowledge of ISP businesses was technically very limited. Worse, I had never worked in any industry, nor did I have any business experience. All my life had been spent in schools and for the first time, the world laid open before me, wide and waiting, to crush or escalate me. I was not protected by the school system, which had a firewall to keep everyone safe but only allowed one to see the world through a window. Now the wide world had become a reality, and I was part of it. No body could help me and no body would guide me. The first step was most scary and frightened but I had determined to make the move. I'd be startled to find out that the ancient Chinese saying – "By deep knowledge of principle, one can change disturbance into order, danger into safety, destruction into survival, and calamity into fortune" – was not the gossamer of dreamers, but real, concrete, paractical advice in the business world.

I had a fairly strong background in science and I understood the basic principles of data communication. To get started building the business, I first worked on the technical issues because without the actual realization of the technology infrastructure, everything was just simply 'talking' and 'talking' was always cheap and easy. I asked myself a few questions. *How could I connect a machine to the Internet? What were the principles behind them? Why was Internet communication so much cheaper than telephone communication?* I searched the Internet on the topics. Little by little I grasped the mysterious art of data communication. I understood now Internet communication was cheap because a message was broken into smaller units called packets, which could then be routed around the world; unlike telephone communication, no dedicated connection was required between the two communicating parties.

After I had straightened out the theoretical part, I made a few calls to the local phone company and a couple local Internet Service Providers (ISPs). Then I had a complete picture of how an ISP worked. I put in an order to the phone company to setup the communication infrastructure. A week later, the phone company dug a big hole in front of my house to install a T1 line and 20 ordinary phone lines. I converted two of my 486-PCs to servers, one running Windows NT Workstation, the other Linux. I purchased 20 new modems, a router, and a CSU-DSU (a device for protecting the router), which were the gateway of my system to the Internet.

As I was a Windows NT fan, I later published two articles in a Windows NT magazine discussing about using NT to provide Internet services. From time to time, my knowledge on technology gave me an edge in running the business. The knowledge gave me good guidance in purchasing equipments or making plans. Without it I would be working like seeking in the dark. It is like purchasing stocks where if you can look beyond the P/E, and P/S ratios to learn the fundamental and technical factors, and read the financial statements of a company, your chance of making money from the stock will largely increase. Even if you are not involved in any business, knowing some fundamental physics and engineering laws makes your daily life a lot more colorful and fun. Unfortunately, technology know-how was not enough to make a business successful. I found out this later.

After setting up the system, I distributed fliers about my dial-up service to the nearby residence; advertising in a newspaper was too expensive for my little company. The response was not as good as I expected though each user was charged for only $14/month for unlimited access, significantly lower than the corresponding charge by big ISPs like AOL and CompuServe. A month later, because of the unfavorable response, I cut the dial-up phone lines to 10. Still, the total expense including the bandwidth fee and phone line cost was about $900. Each month, only about 10 new customers were added. This meant that at the beginning I was losing a few hundred dollars a month which was a lot to me as my saved capital began to dry up after purchasing the communication equipment and setting up the T1 line. Now fear began to creep into my body, might be into my soul. Never did I experience the emotions peculiar to those days, that strange excitement-despair alternation of mood, more powerful than taking university entrance exams or applying promotion in my job.

I could never imagine that coaching a customer to setup a dialup account via the phone was so difficult. Windows 95 was still in the infant stage and many still used Windows 3.1. There were numerous brands of modems and Windows only supported a limited number of them. Many people had no idea how to surf and what did it mean by 'browsing a web site.' Very often, it took more than two hours to explain the details to setup an account properly. I had to answer all the inquiries including both business and technical questions. Often the hard work was not compensated by money but by a wonderful and elevating feeling of successfully connected a customer to the Internet. When such a connection was made, a feeling of satisfaction and pleasure would creep over me and I felt well pleased with myself. Alas, I spoke English with an accent and sometimes that caused troubles. In the process, I found out something very interesting, something that broadened my view of the world. Because I was an employee, working for an income, most of the time, I was served by others in cases like applying for a loan or purchasing a car. Now, I was on the other side of the table and I was offering services to customers. There was a significant difference between serving and being served. Some examples.

Once, I was in a restaurant. A waitress asked me, "Do you want super salad?"

"Yes, I want super-salad."

"Super salad?"

"That's fine. Super-salad."

"Sir, you can only choose either soup or salad."

Finally, I figured out that she was asking me if I wanted soup or salad.

"Soup. Sorry, I thought you were asking me if I wanted super-salad," I apologized.

She burst into laughter but said politely, "Oh, that's cute. You are wonderful!"

So if people want to get money from your pocket, do not worry that you speak with any accent. What would it be like if you wanted to get money from their pockets?

A customer called. After a brief introduction, he asked, "What do I need to buy?"

I answered, "Netscape."

"Landscape? I couldn't understand." He hung up.

Once, I had spent two and a half hours to guide a customer to connect to the Internet but she still could not get what I expected. Finally, I said, "Are you sure that your modem has been turned on?"

She replied with a puzzled voice, "Modem? What is a modem?"

I was almost shocked but I went on to explain, "It is a modulator-demodulator that converts digital signals to analog signals and vice versa. You need the device to access the Internet."

"I don't know what you are talking about." She spoke vociferously and hung up.

So, if there was anything unclear, it was always your fault.

This was new experience to me. I had some colleagues who were pretty rude to book buyers and called them 'human parasites.' Some friends were rude to sales persons and were always annoyed and upset when they were approached by cold-call sales. When I now encountered this usual kind of businessmen, sales, book buyers, and janitors, they no longer seemed alien to me as they once had. I might not understand or share their thoughts and views, but I shared with them life's urges, desires, fears and emotions. I began to console myself: "Even if I lose everything in the business, the experience of gaining a better perspectives of the world is still worth starting it." But deep inside, I knew that I didn't want to be a loser.

The difficulties, which I experienced in my business did not arise so much from my knowledge about the Internet technologies. After all, you could always find all the technical information you need to setup and run an ISP business from the Internet. The most difficult thing for me was to continue to give technical support to beginning users patiently. There were times that I wanted to quit answering technical questions. However, the fear of being a loser stressed me and drove me to work harder to get more customers, which meant more supporting endeavor. When I could not bear the stress and disturbance any more, I withdrew into meditation. I took a deep breathing and recalled my encounter with the fisherman. I found the meditation brought me relief, relaxation, and a return to good benevolent powers. It was this very contemplation, care and exercise of the spirit, which carried me through the tough times. Over time, people requesting dial-up services gradually increased. The web hosting service, which had been only a testing bed at first, began to attract more customers and developed into a crucial component of the business. Six months after its foundation, the company finally 'broke even' and eventually made a 'profit' of slightly less than a thousand dollars a month. The profit was disappointed but was significant to me, as I wanted to save some money to move to an area with much better air quality. What's bad was that the profit did not come automatically. I had to work hard to keep the profit as customers came and went and setting up a new account was a painful task. The technical support was also time consuming. I was earning minimum wages.

I suddenly discovered that I ran into a structural problem. If I could hire someone to do the technical support, I could pay him minimum wages and expand the company. To hire someone, I must first expand the company to generate enough revenue to pay the employee. But without someone's help, I could hardly expand the company. So this became a chicken-and-egg problem. On an hourly basis, I could make a lot more money by working for other organizations. This meant that the more time I spent on the business, the more money I lost. In view of these, I later taught Windows NT in an institute which enabled me to earn extra income at a much higher rate. At the surface, the part-time teaching was a much better job. What I didn't recognize at that time was that I fell back into the trap of what people called "working for money." Instead of minding my business, I spent effort to make more earned income and got trapped in the rat race.

The computer mouse might be the worst technology ever invented in human history. It caused users all kind of back pains and muscle injuries. Unfortunately I had no choice but to live with this devil for many years. The stress and intensive use of the mouse took my toll. After I started the business for a year, my cholesterol level shot up by thirty percent. Gradually, I developed a back pain syndrome. Sometimes, my neck and back were so painful that I could hardly turn my neck and could not fall asleep. Worse, my fingers were getting numb. The syndrome was getting more serious as time went by. *What would happen if I got paralyzed and could not work anymore? Wealth does not mean anything if you do not enjoy life and diversions.* I was struck with fear. One time I dreamed I was typing in front of a PC and the PC gradually morphed into a piano. I tried to strike the keys but all my fingers were frozen. I could not move any of them. Then the fisherman appeared and took over the piano and let his agile fingers run across the keys, so that a magical music floated like a white cloud over Big Bear Lake. I was overcome by bitter hatred towards this man who, so it seemed, had inspired me to start the business and had got me into this mess. I was about to pounce him, but the fisherman smiled with a sad and fine gentleness and said softly, "Remember, Fore. You chose this rough path yourself. Nobody had forced you. You are free to do whatever you please and you may quit tomorrow and resume your old life." I woke up sweating. Fear and anxiety had eroded my soul.

I began to search, anxiously searching for a solution. One night, I watched the movie Forest Gump and was inspired by the character. I decided to resume playing ping pong, the game that I loved to play and won tournaments of it when I was in high school but had stopped playing for more than twenty years. Life was in such a hurry. It had been twenty years since I last picked up my paddle. Someone had said that life was like a bird flying through a lighted house at night – it came in through one window and got out at the other; the light it experienced was so short and transient.

I joined the nearby Big Bear Table Tennis Club and played twice a week. The game lets you experience the unpredictability of life, the despair of being beaten by a lower-ranked player, and the joyfulness of beating some one much stronger than you. At the beginning I was decrepit but I learnt through the game that it was necessary for me to get defeated and experience the nausea and the depths of despair in order to enjoy the joyfulness of victory. Its unfortunate that some people try to suppress this kind of feeling and eventually they lose interest in exercising and fall back to their life of obesity. When you are at your middle age, you have to get every excuse to get you exercise. The only drawback of the game is that it is unbalanced as it is played with one hand. To remedy this defect, I practiced using alternative hands in different games with my right hand against stronger players and left hand against weaker ones. It did not take long for my health to improve and eventually the back pain went away.

Soon after I started playing table tennis, I met various kinds of players, some with very unique character. There was a tall handsome gentleman who came to my attention. He had a moderate belly and I guessed he was in his late thirties, a few years younger than I. In his appearance, he tried to distinguish himself by dressing expensive sports clothes and shoes, and he always kept up with the latest model of paddles of the month. Armed with the best paddle around, he liked to challenge the two best players in the club. To his dismay, the two top players always beat him. Each time when he was defeated, he yelled and scolded himself stupid. On the other hand, he looked down upon players he had beaten. His actions and game were determined less by fun and entertainment than by aspirations and the desire to win. "Your countenance reflects your mind and your mind changes your countenance," a Chinese proverb says. Quite often, we can briefly tell the character of a person from his or her appearance and I had the impression that this gentleman was an arrogant guy, a guy who thought he knew all the answers. It seemed that he would never gain happiness until everybody was below him. I saw him very often but we never played each other. One day, I approached him and we had a chat. He spoke fairly fast. He told me his name but I forgot it almost at the instant he told me.

Then he told me that he had just started a Web-hosting business and asked if I could give him any suggestions.I was excited to find someone in the club who had the same interest as me besides ping pong. I asked, "What kind of machines do you use?"

He said proudly, "I use Pentium machines running Linux. It took me quite a while to learn the necessary details of the OS. Its tough for me."

I said, "If your business is Web-hosting only, I would suggest you switch to Windows NT. It is a lot easier to use; it has a much better kernel and it supports multi-processing. Linux still uses the traditional bulky UNIX kernel instead of a micro kernel like NT and it does not support multi-processing. There are many other contemporary features of NT."

A Modem Pool

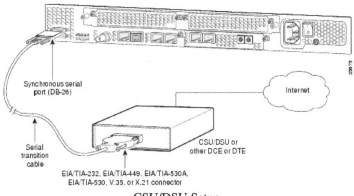

Synchronous serial port (DB-26)

Internet

Serial transition cable

CSU/DSU or other DCE or DTE

EIA/TIA-232, EIA/TIA-449, EIA/TIA-530A, EIA/TIA-530, V.35, or X.21 connector

CSU/DSU Setup

An Adtran CSU/DSU

# Chapter 4    Clash of The Fans

"Allright, come on." He said emotionally.   "I prefer not to start the business if I have to use NT to do it."

"My dear fellow, whatever you prefer, I simply speak of my experience of using NT. It has been working great for me. I would call it 'the OS of the Century'. I really suggest you switch to this OS if you are serious about your business."

"Truly, sir," he said, with an obvious irritation in his voice. "I thank you with all my heart for your suggestion. I wish I were in the position to love Windows but unfortunately I see it as a devil!"

There we began an emotional argument. He thought that NT was trash and Linux was gold but I found that his knowledge on computer science was fairly limited. For most of the time, his argument was based on faith rather than technical context. After arguing for a while, he said, "Great power comes great responsibilities. The company that makes Windows lacks basic integrity. You can deceive some people forever or all the people for a short while but you cannot deceive all the people forever. They abuse their power and break the law frequently. This has been proved and the courts found them guilty time and again. Because they have monopolized the market they can raise the price of the OS products. They bundle any software product that may compete with them and raise the OS price. The cost of the Windows OS is significantly higher than its prior ones."

I said, "But the Windows OS is a lot more complex now. So the price raising is justified."

"It is true that Windows is more complex than DOS but so do the microprocessors, the hard disks, and the graphics cards which are orders of magnitudes more complex than they were ten years ago. Before the monopolization and bundling, the DOS OS contributed to about 5% the cost of a PC but now Windows can cost as much as 1/3 of the total cost of a PC."

In this aspect, I pretty much agreed with him but for the sake of arguing, I said, "But they had clarified that they did nothing wrong."

"So did the former boxing champion. He was found guilty of raping a teenager and was sent to jail. When he got out of the jail, he said the same thing that he did nothing wrong despite the fact that it had been proved beyond doubt that he raped the girl," said the gentleman, laughing loudly.

Again, for the sake of arguing, I said, "As they said, sometimes the law could be unfair."

He chuckled. "The law has never been perfect and has never been as one-sided as it is now," he said. "We are a very rich nation. You know, the one who owns gold makes the rule of gold. We set all the rules of gold."

I didn't quite get what he meant. He paused for a moment and continued: "They think that the law is fair when the law enables them to make billions but the law becomes unfair when it requires them to give others' chances of making millions or causes them to make a few millions less. The government has been subsidizing the company by spending tremendous amount of resources to enforce the intellectual property law to protect their products. The law could have asked them to pay the enforcement fee or could have asked them to use technological methods to take care of any illegal copying themselves."

I protested: "I agree that the law is not perfect but it takes time to make it perfect if it can ever be so."

He shook his head again. "As a nation, in the name of protecting our intellectual property, we tax everybody who directly or indirectly uses this abstract thing the same amount in the world whether he or she is from a rich country or a very poor country," he said. "I have no objection to that. But do you ever know that many of our expensive patented inventions are derived from third world know-how? Do you ever know that our big corporations utilize many vegetation species grown and planted in Africa for generations to derive fat profitable medical or health products? Those countries do not get paid a dime though the commercial products are derived from their intellectual properties. Do you ever know that on the average, each of us pollute the air many times more serious than an average Indian or Chinese? You may say that these are too vague and too complex to argue on. But what if a region uses Windows as their propriety OS and suffers a virus attack which causes loss of billions of dollars in economic damage? It is definitely fair to ask the company to make compensations to the victims. Unfortunately, our law does not require them to do so even though when an oil company spills, it has to pay billions to clean up the environment."

Almost like an instinct reaction, I argued, "If there's a virus attack, shouldn't we blame the hacker or the careless administrator?"

He laughed again and said, "If you bought a house and any thief could easily break your door's lock to steal things from you, do you blame the builder or the thief? If you bought a house and in a rainy season, the rain could leak through the roof, do you blame the rain or the builder?"

He raised a point that for an instant, I did not know how to answer.

I tried to calm myself and said lightly, "I would blame the builder and ask for compensations. Obviously, the builder has not done things according to standards."

He said with a triumphant tone, "Yes, that's obvious but there are people who argue that you should blame the thief and the rain." He paused for a moment and continued: "If they have followed the standard and have listened to advice from security experts, many of the virus and worm attacks could have been avoided, much of the economic damage could be minimized. Its the greed of grabbing more power, the greed of monopolizing the market, the greed of enslaving others that make them to set their own rules instead of using the well-studied agreed upon standards. If they can gather enough followers, they can then further enslave others and monopolize the market. They know that the law is on their side and they have more money than the government to spend on lawyers. They know that they do not need to pay any compensation to victims for damages caused by their irresponsible deeds. They dream that they are innovative but in reality they are just trash, the lowest of the low. They poison this country and pollute the world. If something is not done to stop the pollution, America is destined to become a victim of its own success."

I tried to be sententious but the guy became more livid with excitement. Though I felt that he was garrulous and obstinate, I didn't expect that he could argue so forcefully. He raised some questions that I never thought of before; I mainly concentrated on the technology side of the systems. I did not want to get further into the philosophical arguments and therefore I directed our argument back to the technical merits of the systems. In this aspect, I was a lot more knowledgeable than he. He had difficulties to defend Linux in front of me. Failing to convince me that Linux was more superior, he looked more irritated and finally said, "Well, if you want to spend the rest of your life to work for a college dropout who does not know any programming beyond BASIC, that's your choice."

I felt offended. I made a dreadful effort to control myself and fought for words. I said, looking past him, "We always live on the possession of others. Everyone gives; everyone takes. The merchant gives goods, the teacher instructions, the reporter news, and the ISP Internet services. We are all created equal and we are equal regardless of the nature of our occupation. I never consider the status and contribution of the president of a University is any greater than that of a professor. You are not choosing a technology based on technical merits but on the assumption that there are hierarchy and casts in humans and that employees are at a lower level than employers and the poor are lower than the rich. Your mind set has limited your choice and your freedom of choice. It is your emotion that makes you your own prisoner, prevents you to reach out to the world to utilize the best resources and technologies. You better open your mind to get out of the prison."

Shrugging his shoulder, he shot back: "Well said. I have my mission and I seek my destiny. Some people like to put their destiny on others' hands but I like to control mine. To live a life dictated by the policy set by a few people who abused and misused their power from time to time is not really a life. I don't like to yell at people and I don't want to be yelled at. Sometimes, I do what I have to do but most of the time I do what I am interested to do. It is the urge of this freedom that drives me to take the difficult route. God prepares abundance for all of us and all of us can live with dignity and be rich. I am not saying that my choice is better than yours but this is my choice and my reality."

I collected my thoughts to make an argument:"But isn't it true that you are casting people and you can only work with certain casts and the technologies invented by the people you like?" Recalling from what I read from books, I added: "I guess you need to open your mind to new content or information. You cannot pour more milk into a glass that is already full of milk unless you first empty the glass. It is also impossible for you to accept something new if your mind is closed or already filled with other content. Windows NT is going to conquer the world and you better master it before others do. Your future will be much brighter if you open your mind rather than pretending to know all the answers."

He said vociferously, "The thought of putting people into casts never occurred to me. It is not for me to judge another life. I must judge for myself and make my own choice and rejection. If I were one of those Windows fans, I fear that I would deceive myself that I was developing technologies and attained the purpose of contributing to the improvement of the Internet. I would be just opening another grocery store, making the rich richer, the poor poorer. I don't mean running a grocery store is anything bad, but I am more interested in computing technologies."

It seemed that neither of us would accede to the other's argument. At a point, he glanced at me with a disgusting look in his arrogant face. He acted as if he were spitting at me. I could no longer suppress my anger. His action compelled me to hate him. I tried to calm and tell myself that there's no point to argue with people who ask for advice but don't want to take any advice you're giving them. They have a preprogrammed mindset and could never accept opinions with different perspectives. I ended the discussions abruptly and went on minding my own business. I said, "I hope you are not mistaken in your reasoning. Lets see who will be right and who will succeed in his business. I do not appreciate your arguments but may you reach your goal and I wish you good luck." Picking up his paddle, he said, "Thank you for your advice. Certainly, we will find out who will prevail. May I challenge you now?" "Definitely!"

We took a table. He was significantly taller and stronger than I. We played 21 points, the best of three. The match became personal. This guy has robbed my esteem, I thought. He came to ask advice from me but trashed all my opinions. He trashed something that I valued. Never had I met someone who despised my opinions so much. I wanted to beat him very badly to shake off all of my disgusts. I wanted to teach him a lesson to regain my dignity.

I served first. I threw the ball high into the ceiling and when it dropped down rapidly, I struck it squarely with my paddle, spinning it across the table along with my anger and frustration, content to fall if only my hated foe fell a second before me. Linux Fan did not anticipate such a strong serve and returned the ball high. Immediately, I smashed it with all my energy, sending it to bounce off the table at his side with tremendous speed before my foe could even react to it. In spinning and smashing the ball non-returnable, it had seemed to me as though, in these actions, I were discharging all the hatred into the cosmic emptiness, extinguishing the fire of anger. For a moment, a storm of voluptuous, vengeful delight roared through my senses, and followed the storm, there entered a second or two strange deep calm. But the smash seemed to bring out my opponent's best and my glory seemed to end after that powerful stroke. Ultimately, I was a defensive style player. After a few more exchanges, I recognized that Linux Fan's game was significantly stronger than mine. He immediately established a lead and the lead was widening. He played aggressively, smashing every ball whenever there was a chance. He smashed the ball powerfully as if he was angry at the whole world. I played an opposite style that I hardly made any offense. My style was to let the opponent make unforced errors and lose. If I had known then what I knew a few years later, I would have taken a different approach. I was limited by what I knew and I behaved accordingly. The fear of losing motivated me to fight and worked hard on every point but it could also get into my nerve and pulled me back from chances. It was a battle of will. The desire of beating him brought out my inner strength and I worked hard on every ball and tried to save any ball that I could save. Unfortunately, all my effort withered under his stormy attacks. He hit winners after winners. I was powerless under his spell. Before I could figure out a strategy to contain him, the first game was over and I was beaten badly, loosing 3 to 21.

When we were changing sides to start the second game, he came up and said with a sweet smile, "It was a nice game. Are you ready for the next?" I could see that he was joyful about his victory. He acted as if he had won the debate on Windows-Linux choices. I felt bad and helpless. My world around me melted away and I was overwhelmed by a feeling of icy despair. He had robbed me and now he further threw a punch on my face and I could not do anything. It was a game that I could not lose, could not win and could not quit. Maybe that's life. There are many things that go against your will and you cannot do much.

My thought was wandering and I reflected deeply, recalling many of the past events in a very short period of time; there were so many sorrows in the world and we couldn't do much. I took a deep breath, attempting to subdue the turmoil in my mind. As I was a Buddhism follower, I sometimes practiced breathing in order to regain composure of body and mind and not to lose myself in dispersion and in my surroundings. In Buddhism, the mind is the root of everything.

He began to serve. Suddenly a silence fell upon me. Unexpectedly, I entered the zone. The zone is where the consciousness and unconsciousness meet, the state where you cease to be totally conscious and totally unconscious. Yet the zone can be realized only when you are completely absorbed and rid of the Self; you become one with the environment. Unless you have trained over an extended period and have perfected your technical skill like some martial art masters who could enter and leave the zone at will, you are not likely to get into the zone even once in your whole life. For my case, it was a total accident. I didn't understand why I could suddenly enter the zone. At that moment, the ball, the table, and the players were not isolated objects but were one reality to me. My action was in harmony with his attack and I blocked his balls as natural as breathing. Miraculously, I managed to turn back the wave of his attack.

With the balls kept coming back to him, he became frustrated and occasionally yelled to himself: "Shame on you!" Gradually, his fighting spirit was dismantled. In the next two games, I beat him 23 and 19. At the end of the match, my chest heaved as if I had finished a marathon and sweat glistened across my face like rime. I was exhausted but a joyful feeling overwhelmed me.

This was more than victory. It was a spiritual triumph so complete that I had not only escaped defeat but I had won a spoil so rich and valuable that I felt lucky that the battle ever came. Now I felt that I had won the Windows-Linux debate and had more confidence in myself. Temptation was necessary to settle and confirm us in the spiritual life. "You played well. Hopefully, I could challenge you again next week," he said with a depressed voice.

"Thank you. My pleasure to play with you!" I said. He packed and left the hall. I was in deep thinking. I might not agree with what he said but I could see from his eyes the passion of life. I knew that next time we met, I would have no chance against him. His game was fundamentally much stronger. My only hope was to beat him in the business.

I took another deep breath and sat on a bench. The noise disappeared in my mind as the fast bouncing balls did from my closed eyes. Some of Linux Fan's arguments began to echo in my mind and now I had more time to analyze them. "The one who owns gold sets the rule of gold," I recalled what Linux Fan said. A few years later, the development of the Internet would provide ample evidence of the truth of his claim. Disney and other media company like Time Warner would have successfully lobbied the legislation of the Copyright Term Extension Act (CTEA) that would extend the term for copyright protection for 20 years to 95 years so that Mickey Mouse would not become part of the public domain in 2004. Napster would have lost its lawsuit despite its ingenuity of defense. Amazon and Priceline would have patented the "one-click-button" and "name your button" business methods that are something a little more than trivial.

I did not recognize then the real significance of the statement. There were gorgeous theories and arguments saying that intellectual property should be strongly protected so that the owner could reap the benefits derived from it. Without this incentive, no body would have any interest to develop and invent. The world had been driven and advanced by our greed.

Suddenly, I was submerged in a lonely feeling. Some years ago, a silly Westerner called Joseph Needham spent great efforts to do some stupid things that did not bring him much fame and wealth. He just wanted to answer a question. A few hundred years ago, China was the most technologically advanced country in the world and it had been so for thousands of years. But why did China's technology come to stagnation for a few hundred years while the Western World advanced rapidly? Needham spent his whole life to answer this question. He searched through numerous historical Chinese literatures to seek the answer. After reading thousands of those books written hundreds or perhaps thousands of years ago and making careful analysis, Needham came to the conclusion that Chinese science was based on utilitarianism – people were eager to study and develop something only if they felt that the results were useful; on the contrary, Westerners studied science out of curiosity; they did not care if their results were useful or not. Would there be anyone with my culture background as silly as Needham, spending his whole life to check if Needham's answer was correct? Certainly not me. I wanted to get rich. I wanted to reap the fruits of my efforts. With the emergence of Internet, would greed and the utilitarianism-based intellectual property protection acts bring us to stagnation or would curiosity triumph and take us to a brave new world? I felt bad about myself but at some point I had to make a choice. That's life.

Siliconeer Linux Supercomputer

Logo opposing "Mickey Mouse Protection Act"

# Chapter 5   Windows, Windows!

Next day, I went to see my friend Mike who was also a Windows fan and conducted a Web-hosting business using Windows NT. Mike was a very smart and intelligent renowned thinker in his middle thirties. He was a prodigy of learning who earned a Ph.D. degree in engineering before he turned twenty-four and had won academic awards and prizes. He now worked full time on his Internet business. He didn't at all look like a businessman conducting a business, but rather like a scientist investigating problems of his own. He seemed too superior and detached, his manner too provocatively confident.

When I arrived at Mike's house, he was working on a project using a PC that was running Windows NT. I knew that Mike was a die-hard Windows fan and I did not want to say anything bad about Windows in front of him. I sat next to him to watch his work and I was much astonished. A beautiful dynamic scenery of nature appeared on the PC screen. Mike made a few clicks of the mouse. I then saw a road leading to countryside. The far side scenery was moving towards us as if we were driving in a car along the road. Here and there along the way it was lined with woods, large green pastures and wheat fields. The closer it came the country, the more it passed barns, dairy farms, and gardens. The world seemed to consist of small hills, pretty valleys, meadows, woods, and farmlands. The road eventually ended at a country house and the features stopped moving on the screen. Some fine soft music drifted over from the PC speakers, which were placed underneath the table. The music was so delicate and exquisite that I first thought it was produced from a sophisticated musical system.

Mike made another click and the house interior was displayed as if we had entered the house. I now recognized that he was using a software package based on VRML (Virtual Reality Model Language) to design and create a house. Slowly, he dragged the mouse. The house began to rotate smoothly and more fine features were displayed. Colorful and gorgeous, the stairs, the fireplace, the kitchen, the windows and the furniture all appeared on the screen in proclaimed order. Mike had begun to study I-Ching while he was attending high school and his art design fully reflected his underlying knowledge in the subject. The house was fine and savored with wealth and luxury. Each room was of seemly dimensions and was tuned to a pleasant harmony of a few colors. Here and there were decorated with art treasures and all these rooms, pictures, vases, and flowers seemed to lead ultimately to life of vain longing for harmony and beauty which could be attained only in the preoccupation with harmonious surroundings.

I stared at Mike who was concentrating on his work. A smile and a sense of proud appeared in his face. He certainly enjoyed his work. Windows gave Mike extraordinary power and ease of creating applications to impress non-technical people. But it also consumed him and made him addicted to playing with it, eroding his mind and his soul. He was so absorbed that he began to whisper to himself: "My precious, my love.., my precious ..". He then softly sang about life and the transient of life, about the will to dominate life. It might be the theme song of a certain movie that I did not know of. It was beautiful and gripping how he sang, full of emotion and strength of life. But in his song, life had also become dark, anxious and overshadowed by men's desire for power that caused men to grope around and get lost, until in their hurt, need, and yearning, they tormented and killed one another. While he was whispering and drawing, a tiny bug incidentally settled on his face, sniffed at his skin, crawled a short distance along his cheek, and then stuck to his neck. The movement of the bug seemed to have no connection at all to Mike, who was like a man in deep meditation.

I felt a little uncomfortable about Mike's behavior. Any addiction is bad. Windows had blinded him from exploring the merits of other systems. His analytical skill was deteriorating and his reasoning power declining. But I wouldn't be too worried about Mike. He was so intelligent, and so strong that at the end he would find his way and his destiny.

Suddenly, Mike stopped whispering and singing, his eyes enlarged and mouth half-opened. His face was frozen with this awkward expression for some time. I looked at the screen and immediately understood what had happened. It was the infamous 'blue screen of death.' All the beautiful and gorgeous features were gone and were replaced by a blue screen with cryptic messages. The 'blue screen of death' is a well-known NT feature. It appears when something goes wrong in the system, most likely due to a bug in a software package. It may go away when you reboot the system but it'll come back after you use the system for a while. It has been a nightmare for NT users.

Feeling a little embarrassed, Mike explained, "Actually, the blue screen of death is not a bad thing. It prevents the system from further deteriorating."

Trying to please this proud intellectual, I said, "Yes, the world cannot be perfect. The blue screen of death does not bother me. By the way a tiny bug had settled on your neck."

Flipping off the bug with a finger, he said with a faint smile, "It was a strange bug. So, how is your Internet business?"

I said, "Well, I got some new network applications. You can come over to take a look. Yesterday, I met a Linux fan with a big ego. We had an argument and he really made me sick." I then told Mike about Linux Fan and what he said about Windows.

Mike chuckled. He said, "Those UNIX dummies hate Windows only because Windows has made their jobs look unprofessional. Do you think a UNIX administrator is worth an annual salary of hundred thousand dollars and a database designer or administrator a six-digit figure salary? There is no intellectual context in a UNIX command. The UNIX folks just memorize some commands and pretend that their tasks are sophisticated. Actually, anyone can do what the UNIX folks do. There's nothing to be proud of. It was just by chance in a certain period of history, the demand of those jobs exceeded supply. Now Windows discloses to the world that those UNIX people are not any important professionals. They have long been overpaid. Of course, they are angry and they try to cling to the past and bad-mouth Windows without any justifications."

I said, "Well, I don't have any hard feeling on any of them. At least they posses some professional skills and they are still paid much less than their leaders. I do have a hard feeling about leaders. When you do not have any professional skill, you become a leader and you exploit on others."

Mike chuckled again. "I have met people like Linux Fan before. In my Church, two friends founded an Internet company using Linux servers. They spent all their after-work hours on the system. I just feel sorry for them. Working in the NT environment, I can finish in a day the jobs that may take them a week to finish. In the business world, time is money. If they are doing that for fun, using Linux is fine but if they use it for business, it will just get them nowhere. History has not been kind to stubborn people. Plants are born tender and pliant. They are brittle and dry when they die. The hard and stiff will be broken. The soft and supple will prevail. Some people like to cling to their past and ideals but ignore the reality. They are more willing to attack the giants instead of changing their context. That's why they remain small and will never become a giant," said Mike, shrugging his shoulder. "Well, the garden is beautiful only if it has different kind of flowers. God created a garden that contains numerous flowers. Your friend just makes this world more colorful. I wouldn't be bothered by him."

I said, "Yes, but the problem is that those people think that we are weeds."

Mike said, "That's their problem. They fail to enjoy the garden's beauty. Their gardens are full of weeds."

"You are right, Mike. Thanks for your nice comments, " I said. I nodded and left.

Mike was a wise person and always had his unique view of the world. He's so confident of himself that he seldom showed emotions and would not be bothered by his critics. He was like a lone star traveling along its own path; no wind, no dust could reach it. I envied him for his calmness and wisdom.

Mike's comments restored my confidence in NT. I should ignore what Linux Fan had said. I was almost certain that he would fail in his business. When the day came, I would have the final laugh.

As we were close friends, a couple days later, Mike came to visit me. After dinner, we went to the server room where the equipments of my company were mounted. I wanted to show Mike some new network applications of Linux.

Since the day I made up my mind to start the business, I had practiced the art of networking. In the networking world, everything is governed by protocols, which are rules specifying the way one speaks and behaves. Among the hundreds of networking protocols around, TCP/IP was the most outstanding and the soul of large-scale networks, the protocol of protocols, the rule of rules. It controls the traffic and routes the packets. It gave birth to the Internet, which in turn gave birth to the Web from which dot-coms sprang.

As I logged onto the Linux machine of which I knew the location of every file and program, I found its hostname had been changed. The change struck me with scare. Instantly, I recognized that something bad had happened. I launched a few X-Windows and examined the system logs. New event logs were displayed in real time in an upper left window. I did not know the details yet, but I was investigating. For several minutes I sat tightly and read the logs with great concentration. I recalled a book I read on hacking, "The Cuckoo's Egg", where the author Clifford Stoll described how someone made use of a bug in the emacs program to break into a computer system. It shed some light on my problem.

"What has happened?" asked Mike.

"Someone broke into my system by exploiting a well-known bug in Sendmail and had used an IP spoofing technique to deceive any IP blocking," I answered, switching to another window.

"Sendmail! It is a popular email application that almost all UNIX systems use to handle emails. It is an old and bulky application without any formal documentation; so everyone thinks that it must be good," said Mike, chuckling.

"I should have patched it to eliminate the bug but I was too lazy and too much in distraction," I said, confessing on my carelessness.

"So you just wished hackers wouldn't come. Well, when wishful thinking gives way to reality, life begins to educate us," said Mike.

"The hacker came from a machine located in Russia. Obviously he broke into that machine from another location. I couldn't believe that any hacker would be interested in my system. What could they gain? They should save their energy to hack big organizations," I said, smiling bitterly.

"The Internet world is not basically bright and virtuous but rather is dark and ailing, evil and malign, and when hackers attack, it is not out of please but due to agony. You do not want to conduct anything evil but you have to brace for wicked offenses," said Mike philosophically.

I said, "I shall be more careful but currently I need to undo whatever the hacker has done to my system."

While I was explaining to Mike what had happened, a message popped up on the screen. It read: "Challenging...".

Anger began to boil over me. The hacker broke into my system and now he wanted to challenge me.

Noticing the message, Mike said, "You better unplug the Internet connection from the machine, reinstall the OS and applications, and patch the holes. The machine will be clean and safe."

"This would bring down the system for several hours. My system has too much down time lately, mostly because of the phone company's improper operation of their frame relays, which connect my system to the Internet. I have enough complaints from my customers. Reconstructing the whole thing would be my last resort," I said, sighing. "I have no other choice but to accept his challenge. The hackers have their own code of ethics. If I could beat him, he would not come back to bother me again."

Abandoning Mike's idea of disconnecting the machine to the Internet, I executed in each of three different windows the command *tcp-dump*, which displayed the packets getting in and out of the system along with their identities. Packet data were displayed all over the screen. Like ants seeking food, a wave of packets were rushing into my system, trying to pick up any information that might be useful for further attacks. More dangerously, another group of packets tried to implant a virus, which would replicate itself on the hard disk. I had no time to analyze the nature of all other packets. I immediately launched a special utility command that would intercept specified packets, and insert some special bits into them. The packets would then undergo mutation and their original goals would be defeated. But the packets were coming like tides, wave after wave, flooding my system and making the analysis extremely difficult. I adjusted the system traffic queues to slow down the rate of the incoming packets. In the first ten minutes, I did not manage to achieve the effect of blocking the hacker. I sent out packets after packets through one of the windows. Some carried out the desired mission, some vanished, and some came back to haunt me. My strategy seemed to falter. All of a sudden, I discovered that a virus had been implanted in the system and began to eat up disk space. I was chilled to my heart. Only by that time, did I know that some packets were sheathed under other packets and had escaped my detection. The hacker had eluded me. I immediately launched an anti-virus program, which would sweep the hard disk and kill all viruses it found. If I had hesitated for a moment longer, the system would be ruined beyond repair. I knew that I had no way back. I had to fight on till final victory. I typed and typed; sweat dropped from my forehead onto the keyboard. Never had I typed as intensely as I did at the moment. I lost track of how many commands I had issued. Gradually, the system began to stabilize. The time was ripe to launch a counter attack. I sent out a robot agent to trace the hacker who had to use all means to hide his real identity. The counter attack was effective. The hacking packets began to recede and gradually diminish to insignificance. At the point that almost all hacking packets were gone, a message popped up on the screen saying, "I'll be back, Windows Nut." Then everything came to still and silent. I was surprised to see the message. How did the hacker know that I liked to use Windows? Why did he pick on me?

Nevertheless, the hacker had gone and I breathed a sigh of relief. I readjusted the system queue to increase the data rate so that customers could have better Internet access. The activities were restored to normal. The battle was as exhausted as the Ping Pong match that I fought with Linux Fan. Trying to take a rest, I left the chair on which I sat to type and went to sit on a sofa where I still could see the messages displayed on the screen.

"So, you beat the hacker," said Mike, smiling.

"Yes, he has gone. I am exhausted and need a break," I answered, stretching my legs.

Suddenly, I experienced a pinch at a point of my back. I felt as if I were stung by a bee. Then I felt another pinch on my neck. I knew that my back pain was recurring. It was a classical muscle cramping case. When one is still in a sports game, he will not cramp even if he is exhausted but cramping may occur immediately once he is out of the game and begins to relax. The pain was like an avalanche, which came in a sudden overwhelming rush. In less than one minute, my back, my shoulder, and my neck all hurt seriously. I could not turn my head nor could I move my arms.

I had read a couple books on handling back pain. In a book discussing back pain healing, a national best seller, its author advised readers to ignore the pain, pretending that the pain never exists.

"The pain isn't real. It does not exist. Everything except spirit is based on illusion," I whispered to myself, applying the theory to subdue the pain. In a painful world, the theory had been attractive. But pain had persisted despite the theory and my belief. I felt like falling into a hell. Might be hell was real.

"Let the oxygen flow. Let the blood circulate," I said softly, practicing the book's teaching. I took a deep breath and felt slightly better.

"Look!" Mike suddenly yelled, pointing at the screen. "The hacker is back!"

"Oh, my God," I said, looking at the tcp dumps. The hacking packets were rushing in with more deceiving features. After all these efforts, I was not able to contain the hacker. What should I do? I was deeply disappointed by myself and I almost lost my thought. Should I unplug the Internet cable as Mike suggested at the beginning or should I fight on?

The packets from the hacker rendezvoused and became a worm as if it were a shadow cast by the hacker. The shadow mutated and tended to swallow the system. It swept through the disk and began to seek for cracks to delete crucial files. If only I had my hands and shoulders free of pain, I might launch a counter attack. But I could hardly turn and move not to mention typing commands. Mike was good at Windows but not at Linux. All I could do was to ask him to execute a command to limit the traffic rate to slow down the hacker's attack. Meanwhile I continued searching in my mind, hopelessly searching for a way out.

"Fore, you really should unplug the cable," Mike reminded me.

Might be that was the only choice. Unplugging the cable was basically to admit to the hacker that I was beaten and to signal my customers that my service was lousy. But that was life. Very often, we did not have much choice. Sadly, I had to make such a decision. The sadness and frustrations in me grew and filled me to the point of desiring to quit my business. I sensed my fate.

At the moment that I was asking Mike to unplug the cable, a dim hope flickered in my mind like the dying light of a candle.

"Hold on, Mike. Avogawa!" I exclaimed. "How come I did not think of him?"

"You want to ask help from your friend Avogawa?" asked Mike.

"Yes, he is the programmer of programmers. He can conceive an entire software application in mind. Could you dial this number for me?" I said, pointing at a small yellow sticker paper posted on the wall with my eyesight. I felt like climbing out from the hell.

"Sure," said Mike, dialing and turning on the speaker of the phone. I was struck with nervousness. I just wished Avogawa would be at home.

In a short while a voice spoke in the speaker phone. It was Avogawa's voice. He said, "This is Avogawa. I am attending a national conference and I'll be back next Sunday. Please leave your message after the beep .."

My heart was sinking. My dim hope vanished like the last flame of a dying candle being blown out by the wind. I felt like falling back to the hell. I had rather supposed the fight would be essentially over by the time Avogawa answered my phone. But he had gone and I had no clue where he was.

When I was too much in despair, Mike said, "We may be able to get hold of Avogawa."

"You are kidding. I do not even know which conference he is attending. How could we find him?" I asked with a suspicious voice but my hope was renewed.

"He said that he is attending a national conference. This means that the conference is held in this country. It is quite late now. Any conference session should have ended long ago. Given Avogawa's character, he is most likely working online in a hotel now," said Mike.

"You are right, Mike," I said excitedly. "I can send him an email. As he works with Linux, the email will ring him. Could you type the message for me?"

"Certainly! What do you want to say?" said Mike.

"Urgently need help. Reply to Fore at port 8888," I said. Mike immediately typed and sent the message. Avogawa had an account in my system and I had setup a private talk server at port 8888. If he could receive my message, he would know what I meant and would log onto my machine.

Mike and I waited silently and watched the screen intensely. After a short while, a message popped up, "Avogawa speaking. Fore, what's the matter?"

When I saw the message, I felt like winning an Oscar. Mike explained to Avogawa the condition through the chat server.

"Sent the root password," said Avogawa.

I asked Mike to execute a program that I wrote with a number of input arguments. The program encrypted the root password with Avogawa's public key and delivered the encrypted message to him. In less than twenty seconds, Avogawa logged in as root and took over the control of the machine. I could see that the shadow began to disperse. It behaved as if it were encountering something horrible. Avogawa uploaded a new kernel source and began to compile it. He was fighting the hacker and compiling the kernel at the same time. Such a task was unimaginable to me. The hacking packets rapidly died down. Within seconds the shadow had disappeared, having become one with the darkness and having left no trace of its ever having existed. Twenty minutes later, the machine was rebooted. A message popped up on the screen saying: "Fore, I compiled a new kernel and had patched Sendmail. I cleansed your system, which is now safe and clean. Bye."

Then Avogawa logged out and vanished. He came and went like a comet sweeping across the sky, bright and fast, and then disappeared into the darkness without leaving a trace. This time, I was sure the hacker was completely blocked. Wonderfully strong and happy feelings swelled my heart.

When I began to review the whole hacking process, the disgusted image of Linux Fan floated in my mind.

"It would be too much of a coincidence if the attack was not launched by Linux Fan. He is the one who hates Windows and knows that I am a Windows fan. I remember when he left the hall, his eyes were filled with hate and desire of revenge," I said to Mike.

"It could be him but do not let emotion blind you. As your systems are connected to the Internet, anyone can easily figure out what OS you are using," said Mike, shrugging his shoulder.

"I'll go to Big Bear Club to find him this Saturday. I'll straighten this out with him," I said, my eyes glittering.

"Fore, you are running an Internet business. The last thing that you want to do is to offend a hacker. Just keep a low profile until you are rich," said Mike.

"He compelled me to hate him. He was the one who initiated the debate of Windows-Linux choice. My heart will never be at ease if I do not even this out with him," I said emotionally.

Mike shook his head. "If people came to complain Windows or reproach me in regard to Linux operations, I just listened, let them be

right, and concede to them. In my former company, my colleague Alice
once told me that Windows is garbage and Linux is the crown OS," said
Mike, smiling faintly.

"What did you say then?" I asked.  "I said, 'You are right,'" said
Mike, shrugging his shoulder.

"Really? I thought you would be real upset, " I said.

Mike chuckled. "No way. The other day, another colleague, Bob
commented to me that Linux is junk and Windows is gorgeous," said
Mike.

I asked again, "What did you say this time?"

"I said, 'You are right,'" said Mike, smiling.

I was puzzled by his answer. How could both Alice and Bob be
right?  Mike chuckled again. "Then a third colleague, Cathy heard
about my comments and argued that Alice and Bob could not right at
the same time."

"What did you say this time?" I asked.

"I said, 'You are right too,'" said Mike.

"So actually, you don't care about their comments," I said, laughing.

"You are right. Who cares which OS is the better? There's no point
to argue. What you want is to be successful, to be rich. Once you are
rich and have power, people have to say what you say. They have to do
what you ask them to do," said Mike.

He chuckled and left.

I again abandoned Mike's idea of going easy. I went to Big Bear
Club on Saturday, the day that Linux Fan always came. I purposely
looked for him but he never showed up. This further convinced me
that he conducted the attack. "The thief has a timid mind," a proverb
says. He dared not to come to face me. He dared not to come to answer
me. He was beaten by me in table tennis and beaten by my friend in
computer hacking. He should feel shame of himself. I thought of him
with despise.

I was patient. Unless he totally gave up table tennis, the game that
he loved more than anything else, I would eventually find him, either
in the club, or in some other tournaments. He had nowhere to hide.
Week after week, month after month, I went to the club to look for him.
However, it seemed as if he suddenly vanished in this world. Nobody
heard anything about him. My anger about him gradually faded but he
had cast a shadow in my mind that I wanted to get rich before he could.
I moved on with my own business.

In 1999, three years after I had started the Internet business, I was
still not able to expand the business significantly to generate enough in-

come to hire someone to help. The competition was heating up as there were a lot of free services around and I was tired of doing the dial-up technical support. I spent more and more time to teach Windows NT to get extra income. I finally saved enough for the down payment to move to an area with much better air quality and education environment for kids. I closed my dial-up business that had to be run in my old house. The servers were moved to my ISP for co-location and I concentrated on the web-hosting business. The expensive communication equipments like the router, CSU-DSU and modems all became junk. But I believed that by concentrating on Web hosting and other Internet services that do not require intense technical support, I could do better. I still believed that I could handily beat Linux Fan and at the end, I would do much better than him.

At about the same time that I discontinued my dial-up service, Avogawa and another old friend, Michelle and their families from the East Coast came to visit me.

Image created using VRML

Interior design using VRML

# Chapter 6  The Empire

Avogawa was a counterpart of Mike. He was a die-hard anti-Windows computer professional who helped me fend off a hacker's attack a couple years ago. I did not want to say anything good about Windows in front of him. But Avogawa possessed supreme skill in programming. He could compose complex codes in his head like a musician composing songs. He was also a very interesting person, who liked to talk in a spiritual and philosophical way. When he spoke, he was in every respect different from all the others, was entirely himself, with a personality all his own which made his speech hard to comprehend. Only his close friends could fully understand the messages he wanted to convey. Some of his behaviors might resemble that of Don Quixote who treated windmills as giants and prostitutes as fair ladies. I thought of him as he was – debonair and splendid.

Avogawa brought a laptop along with him. After breakfast, we sat around a table in the patio while he turned on the machine. It was a dual-boot machine, which could either boot to Windows or Linux. While he first booted it to Windows, Avogawa shook his head and gazed at the trees and flowers of the backyard.

Pointing at the garden, Avogawa spoke in his unique and characteristic way, "Fore, everything has a soul. This tree, this flower, and this fruit all have a spirit. So does this OS. But sadly, it has an evil soul, a rotten soul that is full of greed, full of evil, and full of holes for lethal viruses. Many people will suffer. Much economic loss will result."

He sighed, pointing at his laptop. "Last decade was the golden age of computing. Hundred flowers bloomed. Novel ideas sprouted here and there. Each system was bound the power and wisdom to help solve problems. But last decade was also the darkest days in computing history, for everyone was deceived. The Evil Empire secretly fabricated this OS to control all others. They poured all their malice, greed and the will to dominate all life into the OS," said Avogawa.

Avogawa continued to say: "You know, the trouble with rich people is that sometimes they don't care about others. By dumping this OS, which is composed mainly of toxic-waste into the market, they reaped huge profits. But numerous people suffered. I am ashamed of our legal system."

"The other day, the Empire guy came to our company and presented a technical talk on software to the engineers," said Avogawa, his eyes glittering. "Most of us were really upset. We almost wanted to ask him to shut up. He is a salesman. He knows how to sell with all his wiliness but he knows nothing about technologies. If the politicians and businessmen think that he is an admirable person or a hero, that's their business but if he pretends to be an engineer or a scientist, it really makes me sick." He paused and changed tone: "He knowingly speaks, writes and teaches falsehood, knowingly supports lies and deceptions. Not only his deeds violate organic principles, he corrupts the nation's air and soil, its food and drinks; he poisons its thinking and its laws. The consequence is aid and comfort to all the hostile, evil forces that threaten the nation with annihilation."

I chuckled but did not say anything.

Avogawa said, his eyes glittering and tone changed again, "Sometimes, the journalists are brainless. They once asked a well-known Linux engineer how he compared himself to the Empire guy."

I asked, "What did the engineer say?"

Avogawa said, "He felt kind of offended. He just reminded the journalist that he is an engineer but the guy is a businessman. There's another case that a journalist raised a similar question to an engineer who made a big fortune on Internet and had become a billionaire."

I asked, "What happened then?"

"The engineer was upset and reminded the journalist that he finished his Master degree. Of course, the Empire guy never finished his undergraduate study."

I jokingly said, "If someday you become real rich and a journalist ask you a similar question, what would you do?"

"Well, I'll spit on him."

"Come on, that's a barbarian act and you could be put in jail as you would have physically offended others."

"Sorry, I mean I'll spit at him. More precisely, I'll emulate an action of spitting at him."

"Then, the journalist may thank you."

"Why?"

"Because they like controversies."

"Well, that's their business. Anyway, getting rich is not my concern."

Sometimes I felt that Avogawa was like a samurai in the old days or like Don Quixote who followed the narrow path of knight-errantry and despised wealth but not honour. The samurai lived in a world belonged to their own. They had their own ethics code. All wealth and fortune appeared to them as dust and cloud. They did not care if they were kings or beggars. Their goal was to attain the supreme skill in their field like a lone wolf crossing an ice land to seek food. Nothing in the world can threaten them, nothing can be hostile to them. They bear their destiny within their own selves! Such a man loves his destiny and knows himself to be one with it. He carries peace within him.

Michelle had been quietly listening to our conversation. She finally broke her silence and said, "Lets don't worry about the Empire at the moment. Let us see if we could do something more constructive."

We then switched our chatting topic. We had a long chat, talking about the meaning of life and the rapidly changing technology world. Before they left, we agreed to establish a company to provide a certain kind of Internet service. Two weeks later, we founded Happy Web (not real name).

Because of the cost consideration and the flexibility of the available software applications, Happy Web chose Linux as the server platform. Again, like most Internet businesses in those days, Happy Web was losing money. Fortunately, the only recurring cost of Happy Web was the bandwidth fee paid to our ISPs. As we had three founders to share the cost, the loss after deducting the tax was very limited. By the time, I got used to running a money-losing business and the loss did not bother me much. I did not pay much attention to it; it was just another dream that didn't come true.

In the subsequent months, my web-hosting business began to pick up slowly but more and more clients required my company to provide e-mail accounts when they hosted their web sites in our server. Now the cost of hosting web sites using Windows NT became expensive as an NT email server requires a big license fee for just a few hundred accounts and an NT database engine would cost no less. At this point, I had no choice but to convert the NT server to a Linux server. Eventually I chose Qmail to handle emails and PostgreSQL to be the database engine, both of which are reliable and free.

By switching to Qmail, I had a lot more flexibilities in setting the fees of email accounts. If the competition got worse, I could handily make the accounts free.

In the spring of 2000, I received a call from my friend Peter who resided in Hong Kong. He was an expert in the area of image processing and held a few patents including one in water marking. He told me that there's a dot-com-madness in the region. Almost any dot-com company with appropriate connections could go IPO. Peter convinced an investor to co-found a dot-com to build a photo website. He invited me to join the company and offered a competitive salary and a significant portion of stock options.

I imagined that if the company could go public, the stock options

would make me an instant multi-millionaire. It would be the quickest
route to get rich and I would have a lot more financial freedom. So it
didn't take me long to decide to accept the offer. I took two years off
from my teaching job to work on the project. I felt for the moment
entirely relieved from all teaching duties and restrictions and ready to
surrender my whole mind to the new impending adventure. Then I
left US in June, 2000, feeling some sadness at temporarily parting my
family who would come to join me a month later, but also in a mood of
festive anticipation, for although I lacked guidance and companions, I
had, on my own initiative, scrupulously undertaken the new adventure
as a continuation of my pursue of the Internet dream and a step closer
to fulfill the promise I made to myself.

Don Quixote by Honor Daumier (1868)

# Chapter 7    Gold Rush

Located in a remote island, Hong Kong International Airport was among the busiest airports in the world and its passenger terminal was perhaps the world's largest enclosed space. Certainly, it was one of the most energy efficient buildings yet created. Refracted sunlight, a soaring arched roof and unobtrusive air-conditioning created a comfortable and natural ambience all year round. Adjacent to the terminal was the ground transportation center where fast transfers to urban Hong Kong could be made via the Airport Express, public buses and taxis. I took the Airport Express which was actually a high speed train running at a speed of hundred miles per hour. I enjoyed the spacious seating, the cleanness and quietness of the compartment while the train was running at full speed over suspended bridges. Through the large clear windows, I could see the boats, the islands and little hills beyond the blue sea, chain upon chain, all the way to the horizon, where islands and sky merged in bluish uncertainty and could no longer be told apart. The sky was gray except for a few small restless clouds, which floated over distant island mountains, holding the golden light of the setting sun for an unusually long time.

It had been more than twenty years since I first left Hong Kong for America. The place was no longer the region that I was familiar with. It had a much better mass transportation system but unfortunately the air was seriously polluted and for most of the time residents could hardly see the blue sky. Twenty years ago, no matter how poor you were, you still could breathe fresh air to maintain a high spirit. Fasting for a short period won't cause illness but breathing in polluted air will. Maybe that's the price to pay to get rich.

After a 30 minutes ride, I changed to subway, which took me all the way to the office where Peter had been waiting. Peter greeted me warmly and I felt that he was a man, young in feelings and youthful in strength, but with maturity that made one feel like home. He could make someone feel intensely honored and abashed, rewarded and stimulated. He was not only a manager but a mover and a shaper.

"Long time no see, Fore!" said Peter, serving tea to me as all other employees had left.

"Peter, happy to see you. Could you brief Hong Kong for me?" I requested, sipping tea on a sofa.

Peter sighed and I noted a slightly sad expression flashed across his face. "As the real estate market crashed, many millionaires who got rich by trading real estate suddenly lost all their assets and had

a negative net worth. Some committed suicide. I found astonishing changes in Hong Kong after 1997, the year Hong Kong returned
to China. In particular, the swift changes in the attitudes of most of
the high-ranked Hong Kong Government officials were unprecedented.
The school teaching media had switched from English to Chinese. The
Hong Kong Chief Executive, like the President of China, being born
in Shanghai had no trouble in speaking Mandarin, China's official language, but all other officials were struggling to polish their Mandarin.
A local joke summarized the situation:

*After 1997, the President of China who liked partying and social
gathering visited Hong Kong. In a large-scale indoor celebration danc-
ing party, the President chatted with the Chief Executive of Hong Kong
who was accompanied by many high-ranked officials. Every body was
in high spirit and greeted the President gracefully in perfect Mandarin
in the noisy hall. The President liked to crack jokes in a party. Everyone tried to participate in the chat and whenever the Chief Executive laughed, they immediately laughed. They acted as if they fully
understood the context of the jokes and were really enjoying the hu-
mor of the President. But in reality, the hall was so noisy that they
could hardly hear what the President said. As time went on, the group
found that they could hardly understand anything the President said.
Some began to sweat and some began to curse themselves for not studying Mandarin hard enough; if there were a hole in the ground that
would allow them to get away temporarily, they would jump into it.
But nobody wanted to fall behind. It was almost like a primary school
guess- the-leader game; they watched the reaction of the Chief Executive intently; whenever he showed a sign of laughing, they laughed
first, loudly. Some even followed up by saying in perfect Mandarin,
"Its funny!" "Its a nice joke." The President liked to insert English in
his conversation. Finally, he spoke a sentence in English. Everybody
could hear it clearly but for an instant every smile was frozen. The
President said, "Dear Executive, after so many years, you still speak
fluent Shanghainese!"*

With government deficit piling up, there were talks not only of freez-
ing civil servant salary increase but even of reducing it. This exacer-
bated the dissatisfaction of many people."

Peter's briefing was astonishing, astonishing and sad, like a drama
with sad ending and now I also became part of the drama.

Our goal was to first build a large-scale photo site and to provide image protection services using watermarking technologies. A watermark
is a secondary image superimposed on the primary image to provide a

means of protecting the image. A watermark can be visible or invisible. The former is a visible translucent image like the logo seal of a company overlaying on the primary image to mark it as the property of the owning organization. An invisible watermark cannot be seen directly but can be detected by algorithms. Digital watermarking can also be used to embed digital codes in cards and has many other applications. We also tried to develop software applications that could detect steganographic images, which may contain hidden messages. The company only had a few engineers. We worked hard to launch the web site. For economic reasons, we chose Linux as our server platform and we developed robust web server modules to process images online.

As the region had been ravaged with the Asian Financial Storm, the Internet brought new hope. The government thought that the IT industry could rescue the deteriorating economy. There were a lot of rumors of the dot-coms in the region. Many, like myself, chased the rumors and came all the way from America to here to help build dot-coms. I encouraged every friend who was unemployed to switch to this new economy. I told them not to miss the opportunity of taking part in the gold rush. And among all the people I encouraged in the region, my brother, Evans was my most honest believer.

Evans was a couple years younger than I. As we were brothers, not only that we physically looked alike, our mentality and personality were similar. We were not particularly stupid nor were we smart. We were just one of those men whom you meet every day time and time again, but you never really notice his existence because he resembles everyone else, like a collective man. Actually, in many aspects, my brother was slightly more intelligent than I. However, he never graduated from a primary school. He began to work before he finished his fifth grade. Both of us went to the same primary school where the students' academic standard was among the worst in Hong Kong. Like all other kids, we liked to play but hated study; both of us ranked at the bottom of our classes. The fact that I could continue my education and he stopped at fifth grade was totally fate. My parents who were very busy in their work to earn a living, had to spend great efforts to push me to study. They were too tired and too much in despair and did not have energy left to spend on my younger brother. They decided to be easy on him. After all, my father was a peasant and he never formally went to school either.

Without worrying about any homework and schoolwork, Evans had a very happy childhood. Ironically, its his happy childhood that made him never lose the compassion of life, and helped him sail through the hard times.

Evans eventually dropped out of school and the lack of a formal education induced him a very rough life. He endured hardship for many years when he did all kinds of odd jobs, ranging from washing dishes in restaurants to wrapping steel bars in construction sites. Then in the 1990s, it seemed that he found his destiny as he became a truck driver and was happy about the career.

In any case the life of a truck driver is presumably livelier than that of a temporary employee doing odd jobs. Unfortunately, with the downturn of the economy and unemployment rate at historic high, he was laid off and had been jobless for two years. He lived on borrowing and was heavily in debt. I was able to convince him to participate in the new economy. I suddenly realized why my brother's image popped up in my mind when I first thought about starting a business on Internet a few years ago. Might be there was a real motive hidden deep in my mind that I would like to help Evans regain an education that he lost in his childhood.

When I first met him after my return, he looked depressed and pitiful. "Fore," he said, "excuse me for spoiling your good mood of coming home. I am in search of work and peace and should like to be like you and to live as you do. As you see, we were born brothers and while you prosper, I have already suffered much and destiny has played many a hideous trick upon me. For a long time, I did the lowest cast of jobs in the society, being scolded and yelled by my bosses all day long. I saved hard to attend driving schools to become a truck driver. Though many considered it a tough job, this was the greatest triumph that I had yet achieved and it transformed my entire existence. But destiny played upon me again and my boss closed the company overnight, still owing workers three months' salaries. Now, I am an unemployed, an outsider that no one in the society cares. I cannot endure this pitiful life any longer."

"Evans," I said, trying to cheer him up. "In these few years, a monster suddenly appeared in this world that many people try to tame. The fighters and the dreamers all try to control and master it, making it their servant. If somehow you could understand this monster, you will overcome the sorrow of the world in yourself and stop your wheel of fear and job seeking."

"What is this magic monster?" asked Evans with puzzled voice.

"Internet!" I said slowly and clearly.

An eyeful of excitement and hope fired up in his eyes. I then convinced him to work on the Internet.

To start, I helped Evans rent a small shop to sell PCs. I spent great efforts to decorate the PC shop. I believed in Fung Shui, which stated the style of a shop would shape the style of the behavior and speech of the owner. The crucial idea was to base the structure and dimensions of the shop on a harmonious ritual pattern: orientation by the points of the compass, the doors, the spirit wall, the relationships and functions of desks and shelves, their co-ordination with the constellations, the calendar and family life, and the symbolism and stylistic principles of the building. Moreover, I organized the items in the shop according to the teachings of I Ching, where I learned that the mythic order and significance of the shop structure made an unusually appealing and charming symbol of the cosmos and of human's place in the universe. The mythic spirit of the shop owner in this special orientation and architecture would intimately fuse with the magisterial spirit of royal customers. Finally, I structured the shelves and desks carefully to form part of the branches of a tree. When a customer entered the shop, she would not be aware of any tree structure but her subconscious mind would extend the branches to a full tree, convincing her that she was entering a tree garden, and giving her a feeling of cosmic harmony and mysterious freshness. Actually, this is the fundamental principle of building a zen garden. After organizing all the necessary objects, I brought in a small plant to decompose any bad smell and an ionizer to clear the air. An ionizer generates negative ions, which are good for health and will neutralize the positive ions generated by PC monitors. We feel the air very fresh after a thunderstorm is because huge amount of negative ions have been generated by lightning. With this harmonious setup, Evans felt comfortable working in the shop for long hours.

Since the day we opened the shop, Evans had a single goal – to become proficient in networking, to become a participant in the IT industry. Day after day, he came to the shop before any customer showed up and went home after all customers had long gone. He learned, while assembling PCs, to recognize the components, to put them in the right order. He learned to understand their functions, until there were hardly any part he did not know, until he could put the components together flawlessly in a minimal amount of time. A customer came in complaining about the frequent crash of the system, and he silently refunded all her money. A customer came in with her virus-infected system, and he gracefully reinstalled Windows for her. He learned something new each time he solved a problem for a customer, and he was excited and enchanted by the new job.

Guided by popular local books on computer, he practiced Windows networking and servicing. Like his peers, he experienced the nausea of the frequent Windows crashes, and the frustrations of encountering the blue screen of death. He saw through Windows the dark side of men. The greed, the malice, and the desire for power had rushed Windows to the market in a hurry. There was so much error, so many bugs for viruses to reside. Someone made billions at the expense of those who lost billions due to virus infection in their systems. The fortunate enslaved the unfortunate. The rich exploited the poor. *Wasn't this unfair? Wasn't this insane?* He was puzzled by the technical world. He occasionally complained about this insanity to me but for most of the time, he was taciturn and kept the feeling to himself. Day and night, he worked and learned. Quietly and patiently he hacked Windows from inside out. If Windows were a devil, he would sleep with the devil. If Windows were poisonous medicine, he would swallow the medicine. The insanity was the last thing that he would concern too much. Year after year, he had been yelled and scolded by his superiors; year after year, he had been pushed and bullied by his employers. In the two years when he was unemployed, he almost possessed nothing. He had lost his friends. He had lost his self- esteem. The world tasted bitter. Life was pain. All he wanted now was to gain back some basic esteem, to be a man again. If he were crossing the sea, he would have made the raft and would have ferried himself.

Bit by bit, he mastered all the networking details of Windows. He repeatedly practiced building and configuring Windows systems until Windows completely consumed him, to the very core of his existence. Slowly he grasped the art of constructing a network and learned how to embed it in the Internet. Gradually, he could compose any Windows networks at will and he was pleased with it.

But he did not stop there. He did not want to work like a restaurant dish cleaning worker again, repeating the same routine work day after day without knowing what's going on and without using any brain power. He had seen how people suffered from lack of knowledge and were enslaved by the Empire. He did not want to become one of them. Now he began a new struggle, a struggle that would ascend him to a much higher level in the food chain or would crush him and send him back to the cycle of job seeking. He tried to learn the real art of computer networking, to understand the basic protocols, the seven layers of the ISO OSI model, and the principles of security. He studied the protocols, the general rules, the pattern on various networks, and tried to discover the relations between patterns and to reduce infinitudes and multiplicities to simplicity, to system, to concept. However, this was a steep learning curve for him to climb. The world surrounded him like a picture book full of inexhaustible mysteries. From time to time, when he attempted to grasp the details of two peers' communication, the acknowledgment and anti-acknowledgment, the timer and the sync patterns, the blocking and non-blocking, he felt exhausted and lost quickly; he found all his understandings and assumptions were in contradiction and more often he was compelled to put the books aside and to get back to assembling PCs or practicing Windows networking. There were times that he felt he finally got the concept only to find that his understanding was again in contrary with new readings and he experienced a feeling of lightness and despair, such as sometimes occurs in seashore, where a seagull glides above water to target a prey, and when it rushes down to catch it only to find that the target is a shadow and is swiftly repelled again. He experienced this gain and loss in knowledge like a mystery within himself, and suffered with it. Every time he plummeted back into the unknown world, disappointed, he thought about asking me to give him lessons, to clear the hurdles, to initiate him into the secret arts of networking. But at the end, he never made such a request, either because he recognized that I was extremely busy or because he wanted to accept the challenge of doing it himself. Instead, he purchased another book, hoping it would untie his twisted understanding. As days went by, his desk piled up with similar networking books.

His persistent effort slowly softened the materials, slowly, slowly, wore down the entrance barrier of learning this art. Every day he conquered a little piece of it, from socket creation and binding to message passing. The more Evans gained ground, the lower the barrier became. Like moving inside a tunnel under complete darkness, he saw an extremely fuzzy distant dim spot, which might grow or fade with each step forward. At first he was not sure if it was light or was just an illusion. But with persistent pursuing, the spot gradually grew into lightness and became the attractor towards the outlet.

One day, when I dropped by the shop to see him, his books on the desk disappeared. His eyes showed a pure, warm, and delighted brightness, so warm that it seemed to me almost childlike. I was swept with a kind of amazement to such an expression upon the face of the same man who showed bitterness of cracking the knowledge code daily.

"You are scintillating, " I said with a dose of excitement.

"May be," he said softly, his voice full of touching thankfulness. For the first time in my life, I grasp the meaning of knowledge, the art of learning. Thank God the light had not dawned on me too late."

"I congratulate you, Evans. I see that you have discovered something akin to the highest state of humans," I said, feeling his radiance of happiness. "Where are all your books?"

"I sold them back to a bookstore at a discount price. I suddenly felt all the information in those books could be shrunk into a few pages. So I only retain a small handbook for reference purposes."

I was delighted by his mood and said, "You had learnt much but there still remained much to learn."

Despite all his efforts, I knew that Evans was not destined to make any great inventions, or to come close to create any new products. He would never publish anything, nor would he patent any idea. He would remain an unknown link in the chain of technology evolution, but a link as indispensable as any other.

Hong Kong Airport Terminal

Hong Kong Airport Island

# Chapter 8   The Shop

Over time, Evans conducted the business in a style that I could hardly comprehend and appreciate but I seldom intervened his way. He regarded every visitor almost in the same way, whether she was a manager or a student, whether she intended to buy or not, whether she understood Windows from inside out or merely knew anything about PCs, whether she criticized him or complimented him. He always seemed to endorse what customers said and embraced them with polite smiles. Only rarely did I venture to question him as I did one day when a cosmetic business owner happened to pass by the shop and made comments on networking.

It was an autumn evening, overcast, cold, the darkness falling early. After delivering two PCs to a customer, Evans and I took a shortcut heading back to the shop. We walked across a narrow path between two tall buildings. Suddenly we were chilled by some cold water poured down from a building. The cold water soaked my hair and shirt; I shivered with anger."Son of bitch," I yelled. I lost my temper and began to curse the person who poured the water. While I was boiled by anger, I noted that Evans was in a happy mood, looking up with a joyful smile. His behavior further fueled my anger.

"Why are you so happy? Wasn't that enough?" I shouted.

He nodded with a smile and answered, "I felt that I had a fortunate day!"

"You call this event fortunate?"

"Its a blessing that the liquid was not acid and we were not hit by a scissor or a jar! So I felt happy!" Evans answered in a calm voice, " Unlike you, Fore, my life is always rough. So I seize every opportunity to alleviate distress!"

"That's an idiot's thinking!" I shouted again.

Evans fell silent and we quickly rushed to the shop. As I was wet, I immediately changed my clothes and dressed like a janitor to help clean the office. At this instant, a stranger walked in. He told us that he was running a cosmetic business but I noticed that the stranger was actually a high-ranked government official as he put away his badge while he was entering the shop. Most likely he ran the business under his wife's name. He wanted to purchase a few network cards but he sat for an hour or so and boasted how he setup a PC network for his business without any prior knowledge of networking. He claimed that the whole story of networking was nothing more than joining two wires together. The whole IT industry was built on hypes to fetch money from the ignorant.

He despised the computing professionals and he despised everything the Internet had brought. He acted as if he were an expert in the field though it was evident that he was a novice and the way he was running his PC network was full of flaws. Evans listened attentively to this man, whose ego was even bigger than Linux Fan's. I felt resentful that Evans did not lash out against those erroneous views. On the contrary, he seemed to enjoy the distasteful comments of this man who seemed to arouse his curiosity; he not only listened with keen attention, but also smiled and nodded at some phrase of the speaker as though it pleased him. Gradually, I could bear no more of his comments.

"Ah Gor, how many network cards do you need?" I asked, showing a little impatience. He turned to look at me, thought for a while, and continued his chatting with Evans. I waited for another couple minutes, then said, "Excuse me, could you be kind enough to tell me the number of network cards you want to purchase so that I can fetch them for you?"

He again looked at me, and kept silent for a few seconds as if he were solving a difficult mathematical problem.

"I want to purchase the number of cards that I need," he said, grinning.

I began to lose patience. Borrowing a joke from the mathematicians, I said, "From your answer I can tell that you are a high-ranked government official."

"How can you tell?" he said with slight amazement.

"Because you showed three traits of such a person," I said, smiling.

"What are the three traits?" the man asked with a puzzled voice.

"Firstly, you like to think and take your time to answer my question. Doesn't everyone in your position always think carefully before making any comments?" I said.

"Yes," he said, shrugging his shoulder.

"Secondly, what you said is absolutely right, " I said, slightly raising my voice.

He nodded and said, "I agreed. Then what is the third trait?"

I imitated him by looking at him and keeping silent for a few seconds. "I forgot what the third trait exactly is. Maybe its that such a person is knowledgeable and has a touch of zen behind his speech," I said, grinning.

"Nice to know. I'll find out from my colleagues. I forgot to bring money today but I'll purchase the number of cards I need in my next trip," he said laughingly and left.

After the man had departed, I asked Evans in a slightly emotional tone almost of reproach: "How could you have listened so calmly and patiently to this IT idiot? Weren't you wasting your time? It seemed to me that you not only listened with patience, but actually with consensus and a certain amount of appreciation. How could you fail to oppose him? Why didn't you try to refute this man, to strike down his errors and tell him that his PC network thus built is unstable and is extremely vulnerable to worm attacks and virus infection?"

Evans smiled faintly, showing a sign of slight nervousness, and he replied: "I did not refute him because it would have been useless, or rather, because I was not in a position to do so. In eloquence and in knowledge of technology, this man is by far my superior, and I would not have prevailed against him. And furthermore, it is neither my business nor yours to attack a man's belief based on the assumption that what he believes in are lies and errors. I did, I admit, listen to this energetic young man with a good measure of appreciation. I enjoyed his speech because he spoke admirably and humorously, but above all because he reminded me of my life, of the way I present to the world. Fore, you are a learned and humble person and you might think that the stranger was garrulous. You have been a thinker and an intellectual, a man full of knowledge and joy, always on track of what is important and effective, never content with the trivial and boastful. You have a framework of behavior within you, a code, a humble and an eloquent way that you expect others to follow. But you have to realize how many paths there are to communication and that the path of being humble is not the only one and perhaps not even the best one. I did feel more comfortable, out of habit, to chat with arrogant people and make friends with them. Unlike humble people, they have nothing to hide and you can easily tell how much they know and what they don't know. When I know a little I too like to show off to everyone and I am aware that you don't like this attitude. Maybe in my whole life, there's not much to be proud of. It is my way, of course, and I'll stay on it. But I see that you, on the opposite road, on the road of knowledge and information, have interpreted this world in a single way. The criticisms on the IT industry, which the stranger chatted about so humorously and pleasantly are not totally without merit. They are representations of doubters of the information era; those people acquire beliefs to which we reject because our fortune relies on our faith of the technology. But for those who have not yet benefited from the advance in IT or perhaps feel left behind by it, their perceptions of Internet, deriving from their life experience deserve respect. Of course, our belief is different, entirely different. But because we believe in the bright future of the

Internet, that does not mean their views are lies and deceptions."

"But our knowledge in the field is far more superior," I said with disapproval and a sign of displeasure. "And the world has begun to reap the benefits brought by Internet. We have to behold our belief and educate those who are ignorant and still speak like living in the stone age. Those who know the truth must fight against the outmoded thinking and put it in its right place."

Swaying his head, Evans replied wearily, "We do propagate our belief and faith in IT and many people have done so. But those others who cast doubt in it have not been overwhelmed by its development, not yet, and it is not for us to compel them to accept it. Did you not notice, Fore, how successful this young man had been in his life and his cosmetic business and how happily he lived in his lore of images and comparisons? This is a sign that things are well with him and he is not oppressed by suffering. There is not much we can say to a man for whom things go well. In order that a man may accept a new belief contradicting his current view, he must first have endured suffering and disappointment, bitterness and despair, and the fire must have burnt near his eyebrows. At the moment, let us leave this businessman in the happiness of his philosophy, his perceptions and his eloquence. Perhaps tomorrow, or perhaps in a year or so, something may happen that will shatter his philosophy and his wisdom; perhaps his network will crash and his company will lose all the crucial data or perhaps he will be beaten badly by his competitors who have taken the IT development seriously and have endorsed it in their businesses. Should that happen and we meet him again, we will try to help him; we will tell him how we have spent great efforts to master the art of networking and its essence, and how the IT development deserves respect, and should he then ask: 'why didn't you tell me this yesterday or a year ago?' we will answer: 'You were too fortunate at that time.'"

After the reply, Evans subsided into a vein and remained silent for a while. Then, he again smiled faintly with a seemingly sorrow, seemingly helpless expression as if he were confessing about his past, as if he were regretting his derelict of the opportunity of receiving an education. Life had educated and shaped him. I imagined that no matter how mean the customer was, she still behaved much nicer than many of his former employers. I was reviewing his speech and began to recognize that we started out with very similar character and life philosophy and had deviated so hugely over time. When we were kids, we thought the same thoughts, asked the same questions and were happy to the same answers. After these years of traveling entirely different paths, our worlds had grown irreconcilably apart and our thinking deviated beyond my imagination. I could no longer read his mind, nor could he read mine. Yet at the same time, I felt a slender and intimate new bond between us began to develop.

As a matter of fact, he frequently argued with me about the art of human communications and interactions about which I had not paid much attention. In these matters, I learned a great deal from him. Before all else I learned that the destiny of mankind was not mere knowledge learned through formal education, and I was not always a superior of him. It is, on the contrary, many-sided, containing multiplicity of things; life is meaningful only if we treat a human as a human, convince with reasons and respects, but not by tortures and jails. After we had started the business, I began to see him not as a primary school dropout, not as an uneducated person whom the society tended to ignore, but as a man at its work, a man who had his own life philosophy worthy of respect.

I knelt down to wipe the floor, and at the same time tried to think of something to counter his argument. As if awakening from a dream, Evans suddenly asked, "Fore, what is the third trait of the stranger that you can tell from his answer?" I laughed and said, "what he said is absolutely useless." Evans also broke into a hearty laugh. When he tried to add more to his saying, a sturdy, tall, and fairly fat man dressed in nice suits stepped into the shop.

I looked up to him and was slightly surprised to find that he was a Caucasian. With a thick black beard and a large belly, he resembled a widely traveled, and cosmopolitan man, gracious and talkative toward everyone who approached him. His manner was friendly, but it was awkward that he spoke in broken Cantonese, the native language of Hong Kong. As I had a hard time to understand his speech, I tried to impersonate Evans and spoke to him in English while I was wiping the floor. I always tried to present the business to customers from the perceptions and styles of Evans; after all, the shop was run and managed by him.

The stranger was from Boston and was a vice-president of a large electronic corporation. He came here to hold usual business meetings with the local employees and wanted to purchase some PC peripherals. After we had chatted for sometime, he asked with curiosity, "Si Fu, where did you graduate?"

Unsure what to tell him, I stood up to wipe a table and kept silent for a moment.

"I never graduated from any school nor did I finish my primary school study. I began to work when I was a fifth grader," I finally said, pretending that I was Evans and was the janitor of the shop.

Slightly amazed, he asked, "Si Fu, I don't understand how you manage to speak better English than my local managers who graduated from prestigious local universities."

I recognized that I made a mistake in impersonating Evans, who hardly knew any English. But at that moment, I could not back off. Waxing the floor, I said, "I learn that by watching American movies."

"I see," he said, smiling. "I'll watch more local movies to learn Cantonese."

"How much does this cost?" he asked, pointing at a USB-connected flash drive, which had the size of a finger nail trimmer.

"Two hundred fifty-nine Hong Kong dollars! Its a hot item, " I said, putting down the wiping cloth and fetching the drive from the display window to show him.

He examined the item for a while and laid it on the table.

"Two hundred fifty-nine dollars each and I need 253 of them. The total is .., " he talked to himself while pulling a calculator from his pocket.

Without much thinking, I said before he pressed any key, "The total is 65527."

He heard me answering, just for a moment then smiled at me with curiosity as he continued pressing the keys to check the answer.

"You are right! It's 65527," he cried with an eyeful of amazement. "How could you calculate this fast?"

"Well, its just a coincidence. Your numbers are special; 259 is 256 plus 3 and 253 is 256 minus 3. So the product is 256 square minus 3 square. Because I work with computers often, I know that 256 square is 2 to the 16 and is equal to 65536. Of course 3 square is 9. So 65536 minus 9 is 65527." I said, smiling.

"And you learned this in your primary school?" he asked with another puzzled voice.

It seemed that I had made a second mistake. I was not sure if a primary school student would know those tricks. To divert his attention, I explained a few more tricks on calculations.

He nodded and grinned. "I see. It seems that you have used divide-and-conquer techniques to do calculations. I didn't know that mathematics is so fun," he said, pulling a piece of paper from his pocket and handed it to me. Written on the paper was a fairy tale describing a riddle.

*Once upon a time, a monkey king named Sun possessed magic power and could cover a distance of a hundred and eight thousand miles in one somersault. He stood on Buddha's palm and challenged Buddha if he could get out of it. The race began but no matter how fast Sun flipped, Buddha's palm extended faster to contain him. Finally Sun recognized that the palm speed was a function of how fast he moved. He stopped and said, "Oh most venerable one, forgive me for requesting a truce and I apologize for all my rude manners and arrogance. Your power is beyond my comprehension and imagination. Look, we are consumed in this race and are tied to it. Let me go and free yourself from the race if I figure out how to get out of your palm." Buddha had listened in silence to Sun's suggestions with downcast eyes. He now raised them slowly to the level of Sun's face, and gave him a bright, firm and warm gaze. Embarrassed and delighted, Sun remained standing in the palm and said: "I now understand how your palm works. I am standing at the center of your palm, and I am one kilometer from the end. I'll move forward slowly. In one second I walk a distance of one meter relative to your palm, and I know that in this one second, your palm extends uniformly by one kilometer. In this way, some day I'll be out of your palm." Sun stepped forward for one meter in a period of one second and indeed Buddha's palm had extended uniformly by one kilometer in the same amount of time. As Buddha watched Sun's movement, pondered upon his solution, his mouth slowly twisted into a smile, then a laugh. Buddha flipped his palm and let Sun go.*

*Why did Buddha free Sun?*

I recognized that the riddle was adopted from one published in Scientific America some years ago. I jokingly said, "Might be because Sun had complimented Buddha. So Buddha let him go."

"That may be so," said Eric, smiling bitterly. "The riddle is setup by my managers here to test the thinking capacity of candidates during job interviews. They sent this to me via email last night for comments. I sense that they have the intention of testing me too. I thought over this riddle for the whole night but could not come up with a solution let alone make any comments."

Feeling that Eric was looking for help, I said in a more serious tone, "Buddha freed Sun because Sun would get out of the palm someday."

Eric received me with an amazed but not surprised look. "Wouldn't the distance that Sun has to cover becomes larger and larger? How could he get out of the palm?" asked Eric.

I explained: "Not necessarily. Each time Buddha extended his palm, Sun was carried forward too. In the first second, the fraction of distance he would cover is 1/1000, the second, 1/2000, the third, 1/3000 and so on. So the total fraction of distance he would cover in n seconds is $(1 + 1/2 + 1/3 + .. + 1/n)/1000$. He would be out of the palm when this fraction is larger than one. But we know that the sequence is divergent. That is, when n goes to infinity, it goes to infinity too. So for sure, Sun could eventually get out of the palm."

Nodding and smiling, Eric said, "Si Fu, you explained well. Naturally, I hope that you are going to tell me all your tricks of learning, but it seems that your learning method is a mystery of art." He pulled a card from his pocket and handed it to me:

```
Eric Finkenthal
Vice President
Nirvana Electronics Corporation
Boston, MA 98264
```

Then he gave me a form and said in a friendly voice, "Si Fu, our local branch will invite vendors to bid for the administration and maintenance of its computer network. I hope you will compete for the contract. I am in no position to choose the vendor but out of respect, they will ask my opinion. In general I would make no suggestion but this time, I'll recommend your company. If a janitor in your company could solve a riddle that I could not solve in one night, I have confidence that it could do a good job in networking services."

I thanked him and wished him a happy trip.

After Eric had left, I informed Evans about the news of bidding. He was cheered up and immediately prepared the information and data required for submitting the bid. I then pushed him hard to learn the Linux system as this would be a basic requirement to maintain the company's network. This was a particular frustrated learning experience to Evans. He hardly knew any English as he never finished his fifth grade. I could learn a command like 'sort' effortlessly as I already knew its meaning as an English word. A command did not appear to him as a word but as a composite of alphabets. He had to scan through the maze of symbols to find its meaning. Learning a command montage was no easy task for him.

At the beginning, Evans was frustrated and felt the pain of learning. Things might be a lot easier if he had started out with Linux. But Windows had consumed him, sending his consciousness to sleep. He did not want to work with anything that did not provide a GUI interface. Even wise men like Mike could not escape from the addiction of the Windows cycle. I had asked my brother to travel a very rough path, a path that he felt he could not advance further. I encouraged him and told him that when he traveled it to the end, the painful suffering would cease to be a festering wound and would become a deserved good fortune, better future, pride and possession. I convinced him that he was able to handle all the crucial Linux commands. More and more people would purchase Linux systems as the software was free. He would then be ahead of his competitors. He would then leave the troubled course of the life cycle once and for all. He was deeply despondent, and yet he realized that I was right. He entrusted me and continued to travel this rough path. Not until a couple months had past, did I recognize that I had led him to another hell. A perfect storm was forming but I was not aware of it.

As Buddha had taught us, life is full of unexpected events. Not long after I had begun to work in the photo dot-com, the Hong Kong stock market began to crash. To many local residents, this was the beginning of another nightmare since 1997. As days went by, the chance of getting the company public became slim and remote. We were forced to change our strategy and worked hard to generate immediate revenue. Hopefully, we could get enough to pay the employees' salaries.

We began to build Linux-based web-database for other companies but the income was not enough to cover the expenses. We tried different other things. One idea was to let customers submit digital photos online and we made high-quality photo printouts for them. But to accomplish the goal, the investor had to pump more money to purchase a couple machines for photo development. At that time, no such business existed in the region and we had high hopes on the plan. Everybody was enthusiastic. We found a life belt in a sinking ship.

In December, one day Peter invited me to have dinner during lunch hours. He left early and I would meet him in a restaurant. On the way to the restaurant, I dropped by the PC shop to visit my brother. The business activities had declined significantly in the past month. It seemed that nobody wanted to spend money on technologies. Hardly a day would pass without news about dot-com dismissing employees. I wanted to cheer my brother up, to tell him that this was a temporary phenomenon.

However, when I arrived at the shop, it was closed and locked. Lights were turned off. I dialed my brother's cell phone only to find that the service had been discontinued. Most likely, he had gone to get some slack. I guessed. Still I worried that he might quit the work as he indicated to me before that he wanted to give up and become a truck driver again. Before I left the shop, I put a tiny mark on the lock.

When I arrived at the restaurant, Peter was there already. After seating, Peter said, "Fore, the local IT market is in a free fall. You can read from the newspaper that there're dot-coms closing or cutting jobs almost everyday."

Feeling uneasy about Peter's message, I said, "I was aware of that but with our company's low budget and the revenue the company begins to generate, we should be able to hang around for at least two years. We could survive this dot-com storm. The investor promised to invest one million US dollars in the company."

"Yes, that's what he promised but he said that unfortunately he allocated the amount of money for the investment in the form of stocks. Each time he pays us, he has to sell some stocks. Recently, he suffered a huge loss in the stock market. He said he could not afford to purchase the photo printing machines," said Peter.

Disappointed, I said, "Without the machines, the company could go nowhere, at least at this moment."

"Yes, that's what the investor thought too," said Peter, taking a sip of tea. "He decided to close the company tomorrow. Everyone including myself will be dismissed. You have to clean up your office tomorrow and leave."

Hearing what Peter said, I sat straight and still. For a moment and for an instant of breathing, my heart was frozen. An icy chill stole over me and I shivered inwardly like a homeless little cat. It was not even half way of my leave. Where could I get the money to survive for the rest of the period?

Peter apologized for getting me into the hot water. I did not blame him. I should have prepared for the worst. If I had not, it was my fault. I immediately planned to send my family back to America to reduce the living expense and I would move to live with my Mom. I believed my case was not unique. There were some other IT professionals who resigned from large corporations overseas and came back for the gold rush. By the end of the year, most of them ended up losing their jobs at both ends.

A couple days later, I purchased air tickets for my family to go back to America. At the airport, I told my daughter that our temporary separation was to position our better unification and better life in the future. Sadly, I said goodbye to them. After they left, I was depressing and went to the PC shop to visit Evans again.

When I arrived at the shop I felt a chill sweeping through my whole body for the shop was closed again. I wanted to know if what I had already sensed was true. So I leaned over the lock and examined the mark on it. I immediately concluded that no body had entered the shop since I put it there. Finally, I recognized that my brother had given up and had quit. He quit school thirty years ago and now he quit learning IT halfway just like the way I quit the ISP business. We were brothers and we were both quitters.

I began to blame myself. *You should not push him to learn Linux. You should have left him having fun with Windows. You are such an ivory idiot. What you have been doing is chimerical. Dummy, he quit school when he was a kid. Doing odd jobs is his destiny.*

Weariness descended on me. It was through a strange and insidious path that I had got into this mess, into a world that had deserted me. Was it really necessary, was it right, was it not a foolish game to get into this Internet business that nobody really knew what it was? Grief and anger was soaring higher and higher, and began to boil over me. I was angry at myself, angry at the world. I suddenly felt mentally sick. Might be seriously sick.

A Zen Garden

A Flash Drive

# Chapter 9   Reborn

I was wandering in the streets, lost in thought. I knew only one thing - - that I was jobless, that my compassion in Internet had led me nowhere, that my opportunity was over and done with. A gentle, cool stream of sadness and spiritual anxiety crept into my heart. I was thirst to swallow any mental medicine that could help me. I took a ferry to a remote island to make a pilgrimage in order to seek peace in my mind. There was a Buddha temple on the top of the island's mountain. I walked alone and depressively along a small path, which zigzagged up the hill. Near the path was a small stream that intersected with it at several locations. Various kinds of old large unknown trees blocked the strong sunlight to provide a comfortable shade for walking. It took me an hour to get to the top. At the end, I saw a large concrete plaza with a few Buddha statues located near the edges. A temple without any window was built at the north side of it.

I sat on a tree trunk to have a nap as I was very tired after climbing the hill. I hardly knew whether I was still awake or had fallen asleep when I heard the faint murmuring of the glittering water from the stream, the hum of monks and nuns, and the simple melodies of the wooden fish, a traditional musical instrument used by Buddha followers. I walked across the square and entered the temple. Embedded on the walls were various kinds of Buddha statues. About three dozens people had gathered there and sat quietly on the floor with legs folded and crossed. They were full of attention, for they had come to be consoled and enlightened by the monks and nuns of the temple.

In front of the people stood a nun of Buddha, a somber woman dressed in gray with intelligent, tired eyes, and pale face, and she spoke with a clear, mild, and sweet voice to the audience. She told the listeners how gods originated long ago in the olden days, out of the needs and wishes of the people at that time, who had not recognized the unity of nature. They had always seen just the single and momentary thing, prioritizing urgent things rather than important things, those primitive people, and so they needed and created for each thing a special god – a god for the sea and the land, for sun and moon, for rain and fire. But in Buddhism there is only one primordial force – the essence of mind, she explained. All else is virtuality. Form is emptiness. Emptiness is form. The nun who served wisdom explained to the audience the Buddhism theories, from the pure, immaculate Dharmakaya to the Satipatthana Sutta, the basic manual on meditation. She introduced the Four Noble Truths, Five Precepts, Six Paramitas, and Eightfold Path, and explained how one could reach the Pure Land, the Nirvana through practicing Buddhism.

One term after another was raised and then elaborated, and each time I felt a small delicate triumph in my mind, along with mild sympathy and peace in my heart.

Looking at the lecturer more carefully, I was astonished by her beauty. She was a youngster with pale skin, which was as smooth as that of a baby. I was puzzled. Why did the temple choose such a young nun to speak on the complex difficult Buddhism theories which would take one many years to master? I tried to straighten this out and all at once I found that I actually knew the lecturer. She was Shalina whom I met before and read about in local newspapers.

The discovery only confused me further! It was twenty years ago when my older brother worked in a local TV station that I met her during some brief visits. She was one of the most beloved TV stars. Then at the peak of her fame she mysteriously resigned and took refuge in Buddha. It seemed that she had not aged a bit in twenty years. It seemed to her as if all the times and ages of humankind had faded and become unreal. A few years ago, a woman at the age of forty-seven entered the Miss Hong Kong Beauty Contest to compete with girls at ages less than half of hers. I thought it was a joke. Not until the moment I recognized Shalina did I believe that a forty- seven year old woman could look like a teenager.

After Shalina had finished the session and the crowd had dispersed, I stepped forward and greeted her. When I looked at her and felt her glance, I saw that she did not recognize me.

I said, "You have shown much kindness to us and have ferried us across the suffering sea."

She bowed and answered politely, "Amitabfa! I have not ferried anybody. If I have done anything, I might have made some rafts. If you have crossed the suffering sea, it is only because you have ferried yourself."

"Each time you elaborated a Buddhism theory, I registered a little triumph in my mind. I felt your kindness and your love. I commend you for your fine job, Shalina," I said, smiling.

Amazed, she stared at me. There was silence for a moment and then she said with a warm smile, "You are Fore. You once assembled and fixed a PC for me. That was twenty years ago. I am joyful to see you again. Amitabfa! I am now Nun Anonymous!"

I was delighted that she recognized me. I said, "You had traveled an extraordinary path. You went to America to study and after graduation, you came back to work in a TV station and then chose to serve Buddha. I read about you in the newspaper. It seemed to me as though it had been only yesterday that you had come to this temple and took refuge in Buddha. You must have your reasons to choose such a path. Have you found your right path and your destiny? Have you acquired enlightenment and seen things beyond life and death?"

She answered with a soft voice, "Amitabfa! After twenty years' effort, I am close to understand life and death but I will not stop searching; that is my destiny."

I said, "I too have studied Buddhism for many years but I feel that I am always at the entrance of the Buddhism World. There are a lot more things that I don't understand than those I understand. Could you tell me the meaning of life? Is life the most sublime and beautiful thing in the world?"

She answered clearly and firmly, "Life is death, death is life, and they are entangled in an eternal furious struggle of love and kindness and this is the ultimate essence of the universe. Buddha had fully understood this and could thus live beyond death."

I said, "That I don't understand. Life is life. Death is death. They are two different concepts. I know that when there's life, there's death. But isn't it true that when one dies, the Self vanishes? I have no doubt that Buddha possessed supreme knowledge but how could he remember his earlier lives and could live beyond death?"

Nodding her head, Nun Anonymous said warmly, "No, the Self does not vanish. As you know, Buddha had reached Nirvana and would never return to the cycle of life and death, never submerge in the troubled river of formation. But Buddha suffered from the development of a language to disclose his thoughts. He himself understood life and death but once his thought was expressed in words, the meaning is twisted. Einstein was fortunate that the language for presenting his relativity theory, namely Lorentz Transformation was ready and mature when he came up with his ideas. Relativity, which made use of the math tool devised for its own ends a theory composed of formulas, abbreviations and combinations and this theory of serial formulas and formulary dialogues were everywhere comprehended by scholars. Without the mathematical formulation, it would be very difficult if not impossible for him to express his thoughts. It is also impossible for one to understand relativity without first studying its mathematical tools."

I nodded while she continued to say: "'Life is death' does not mean life and death are mathematically equivalent. It should be understood in the same sense as 'water is ice; ice is water'. Water and ice are the same substance at different states. In Buddhism, knowledge is regarded as an obstacle to understanding, like a block of ice that obstructs water from flowing. You must go beyond the veil of language to seek the essence of life. Only gradually and unconsciously does the link between life and death become apparent. The link grows closer and more intimate when you begin to sense that life and death are actually different states of a Self."

I murmured to myself, "It sounds like learning COM objects in programming. Only after a lot of study and practice could one sense why people have to build programs in such an awkward way."

I raised a question: "Is it true that everyone has a former life and I might have changed from a horse in my former life to a man in my current life?"

"Yes and no. The change is not a one to one mapping. Every instant we change. The tree leaves change to soil; the soil changes to oil, the oil changes to gas. Every sitting, every walking, every smile will have an effect on your own daily life, and the life of other people. Your word and your deed will give rise to the next state of the universe. Your spirit lives on. This instant is a point in the space-time phase of the universe. It inherits the past and evolves into the future. The concept of state transition is fundamental in Buddhism. Life and death is only separated by a state transition. When you understand the link between life and death, you will recognize that life is the most precious. The struggle against death, the unconditional and self-willed determination to live, is the motive power behind the lives and activities of all outstanding humans. Buddha taught us to find whatever means possible to protect life and prevent war. Do not kill and do not let others kill," said Nun Anonymous, stepping forward and pointing at the stream outside the temple. "Its just like water and ice. Water at ninety degrees and water at sixty degrees are at the same state. They are still water. But water at zero degree and ice at zero degree are at different states. In the same way life and death are at different states."

I was aware that the word state that Nun Anonymous had used was slightly different from its meaning in physics but I understood from her context what she meant.

She suddenly asked, "Do you think if there is a state transition when a baby is born?"

I thought for a moment and said, "No, I don't think so."

"You are right. As a consequence, there is no difference between killing a baby one second after it has been born and killing it one second before it is born," said Nun Anonymous.

"So there is also no difference between killing a baby one second before it is born and killing it a few months before it is born. A human life is killed," I said, inspiring from her explanations. Nodding her head, she said, "Right. But a state transition occurs when a sperm and an egg combine. A human life is formed. If you destroy the sperm and the egg before they combine, you have not terminated any human life. If you do that after the combination, you kill a human life."

In a soft, yet firm voice, Nun Anonymous further elaborated the meaning of life. She explained patiently with examples and repetitions; warm and still, her voice hovered me like the autumn sunlight, like the sea breeze. I felt fresh and rejuvenated. Everything was warm and comfortable. I could hear my soul humming deeply and contentedly like a butterfly enjoying the full fragrance of the air and the spring sunlight.

"Shalina, excuse me for asking you a final question that might be gauche," I said, feeling a little embarrassing. "How do you maintain your youth. You have not aged a bit in twenty years."

With another warm smile, she replied, "Appearance is deceiving but Budha taught us to love our bodies. Inspired by the Japanese monks of Mount Hiei, each day I run ten miles, meditate one hour, stretch one hour and sleep five hours. My life is centered around kindness, avoiding killing directly or indirectly. Leafy greens make up my diet montage, half of them raw, and half of them cooked. For twenty years I have not touched any processed food, caught any cold or taken any medicine."

When she finished speaking, I had a strong desire to hug her, to feel her grace and her kindness. I ran up to her, ready to give her a friendly handshake or embrace her. Then I realized that she had become a Buddhist nun, and therefore no longer an ordinary friend. I stopped short as though suddenly numbed, and moved slowly and respectfully forward and made a low obeisance. She bowed and said softly, "Amitabfa!"

The pilgrimage was like magic. When I left the temple, I felt that I was completely healed though I still had to survive the financial fallout.

When I got home, the phone rang. A friend offered me a part-time consulting job in a game company called Delight Inc. (not real name), which developed embedded programs for electronic toys. At the time, there was a new law passed in Hong Kong that required all companies to purchase legal copies of software. Any company caught using pirated software would be prosecuted and punished heavily. The company urgently needed someone to convert their Windows-based network to one that ran the free Linux OS. I gratefully accepted the offer and next day when I started working, I began to convert all NT servers to Linux servers. The engineers' PCs were also switched to Linux. Only the secretary and the administration department used Windows systems but instead of using the MS Office, they switched to the Star Office, which was free at that time. The transformation was smoother than I expected. Even the secretary adapted to the new system in one day; she had no trouble in switching from MS Office to Star Office and never had any complaint about the new software. I was glad that I helped the company save a significant amount of software cost. The cost cutting was critical to the survival of the company as it faced fierce competitions from companies located in Shenzhen, a coastal city in China next to Hong Kong.

Delight Inc. had less than twenty employees. It was a pleasure to work there where most personnel including the founders were engineers. Everybody had to do hands-on work. The engineers were from local universities and they were just as bright and knowledgeable as their counterparts in America. They studied hard to gain the professional skills when they were students in the University and they applied their knowledge to make contributions to the society. There were thousands of these kinds of small firms in the region. Now I began to recognize that the world was not advanced by a few innovative genius or billionaires as the media wanted you to believe but was built by an uncountable number of people who worked with solid professional skills. These were unsung heroes who deserved praises. It was a tragic that our media glorified and exaggerated the contributions of a small group of so-called 'genius'. The world would move on with or without this elite group but it would immediately come to a halt if the professionals stopped working.

At the end of the first day of my new job, I was physically exhausted but mentally fresh. When I got home, my Mom told me that Evans had accepted and started a truck-driving job, which required him to drive in Southern China to load and unload goods from factories. He would be away from Hong Kong for a couple months. If I had not been to the temple, I might be angry at him when I heard the news. The pilgrimage had rejuvenated me and I felt the warmth of the world. I forgave Evans but I felt sorry for his decision. I knew that he would loose his job again if the economy got worse. Already there had been reports that some traveling agencies fired all their bus drivers and rehired some of them only to cut their salaries by half; no government officials made any comments.

To improve her competitiveness, Delight Inc. established an office in Shenzhen, the fast growing city that had become a brazen and appealing work of wonder. In twenty years, the city had risen from a fishing village to a metro center that dominated the neighboring cities in Mainland. Solemn and splendid administrative buildings and banks, hotels and shopping malls arose on the wide, cheerful streets, where farmers used to grow rice. For the past two decades, the city was venerable, a favorite place for young talents in China, glorified by the government, and visited by dreamers.

Shenzhen was a wild weird world. Many adventures and the way people conducted business were beyond my wildest imagination. One day I walked past a busy cross-section at a highway entrance. Suddenly a scene made me shiver to my bones. A man was holding with one hand the neck of a large snake high in the air. Beside him was a small table with two buckets under it. Opening its jaws wide and wagging its tail swiftly, the snake was struggling to free itself. When the light turned red, the passenger of a car waiting in line rolled down the window and handed the man some bills. Immediately, the snake holder cut off the snake's head and sliced open its body, washed it, cut it into pieces, wrapped them in a plastic bag and handed it over to the passenger. He finished all these long before the light turned green. Life was tough for a road side orange seller in America, but it was much tougher for this snake grocer. I was scared to work in such an environment but I had no choice.

I helped hire in Shenzhen a few more engineers whose monthly salaries ranged from five to eight hundred US dollars. One of the newly hired engineers was graduated from a moderate University in China with fairly good academic results and had two years of working experience. We called him Rabbit because he could run very fast and was agile. Rabbit came from a small village in the middle of China. Before attending University, he helped his parents grow vegetables. In spite of his moderate background and his lack of interest in social activities, his performance was exemplary. He impressed me with his proficiency in designing hardware circuits and programming them using an assembly language or C language. But above all, his most valuable asset that hardly anyone noticed was his analytical skill. In the interview, to test his thinking capability, I presented to him the Sun-Buddha problem I learned from Eric. I was posed to give him some hints if asked. After reading the descriptions, Rabbit did not say anything. Quietly and calmly, he looked out into the dynamics of the busy streets. For a minute or so he seemed to be detached from his environment. Then slowly his eyes returned from the abstraction and received me with a confident look.

He explained: "If x is the length of the Buddha's palm, the fraction of distance that Sun covered in each step is essentially one over x and the total is essentially the integration of it. The integration of 1/x is log x which is divergent. Thus Sun certainly could get out of the palm ... "

I was shocked to hear his answer. In about one minute, not only did Rabbit solve a problem that Eric failed to solve in one night, his answer also gives insight on how fast could Sun get out of the palm. Without hesitation, I offered him the position of senior software engineer.

One time we had a game project that involved calculations of special trajectories of a dynamic object moving on a spherical surface. No body in the Hong Kong branch of the company could solve the problem. A couple engineers worked on it for a couple days but came short of any solution. I used to be good at solving analytical problems but like most programmers, after years of coding, I gradually lost this skill. I thought over the problem for an hour but could not come up with a general solution. The project was stuck at the point and could not proceed further without knowing the general solution for the trajectories. The whole project team came to a stand still. I then took the problem to Rabbit. Miraculously, he solved it in about an hour and the team could resume their work. It was hard to over-estimate Rabbit's impact on the company. Given the small size of the company, the existence of an engineer like Rabbit determined if the company could make a fortune or lingered at the survival boundary. What shocked me most was that before joining Delight Inc., Rabbit worked in a company with a similar size; he switched job because he wanted to earn about forty to sixty dollars more a month. His former boss preferred to let him leave than give him a raise. This was shocking new experience to me and I would hardly believe this would happen in the real world without experiencing it. So the business world was full of excitement and unexpected behaviors. In spite of my aversion to business and personnel affairs, I began participating in management and mixing with business people with whom I normally did not associate. Nor did I like the unavoidable business gatherings and chats even though they were infrequent.

The result was so remarkable that, from then on, I maintained a consulting relationship with Delight Inc., which would continue after I returned to the US.

The salary from Delight Inc. bought me time to explore other Internet adventures.

At first, I formed an online printing company with three friends. The printing company concentrated on services of printing business cards, posters, fliers and small items. The new thing was that a customer submitted the printing content via the Web; our server would configure the material in the final printing format for her approval. Upon receiving the final approval, it would send the context to the print server to make the printouts. All the information and transactions were processed automatically and handled by several Linux servers. We finished building the Web site and the server system in about three months. Unfortunately, the printing machines were too expensive and because of the crash of the stock market and the bust of the Internet, we were not able to raise capitals to purchase the printing machines. Eventually, we mothballed the project.

Then we tried various projects ranging from building digital cameras to developing web radios. But again after months of endeavors, our products did not find much market. Basically, all my efforts spent on Internet products were in vain. It might be the worst period for startups to develop any Internet product. I was disappointed but that's life.

During that period, I met a trader who was a supreme table tennis player. She taught me the Zen of Ping Pong and in return, I taught her the Art of Computing. She told me that I had to play more aggressively if I wanted to improve my game. It was pretty much like investment. Playing safe would not lead you anywhere. She said. One must have different strategies in dealing with different stocks under different circumstances. Also, to advance my skill by changing my playing style, I would first suffer a sequence of unexpected defeats over a substantial period of time.

About a month after I started the new job, one night when I arrived home, the phone rang.

"Hello," said a voice in the phone.

Immediately, I recognized that it was the voice of Evans. I spoke warmly to him, "Brother, what had happened to you? Where are you now?"

"I am in Margaret Hospital. I have been here for three days. I was infected by a virus but I have recovered and will leave the hospital tomorrow," he answered.

I was shocked. I rushed to Margaret Hospital, which provided free medical care to every local resident.

When I saw Evans, he was lying on a bed. His face was pale and looked tired. A feeling of sadness came over me like a stab in the heart.

"Fore, I am sorry to let you down," said my brother and tears started in his eyes. "You were my teacher, my advisor and brother confessor during that very first few difficult months in the shop, and I took away too much of your valuable time. It might be a grave mistake for you to open the PC shop with me."

"I have scarcely ever had a finer investment," I said warmly, trying to cheer him up, "and was then at peace and happy, in a way that one rarely is, with myself. I was truly proud of you and I am still so today. Do you still remember the race you won the electric car from Uncle Seven? I did not recognize then until I entered college that you had utilized the least-time principle to beat us all. Your path was bent as you ran a longer distance in the dried field so that you traveled a shorter distance in the mud and the stream. That is exactly what a light ray would do when it travels from air to water to get to the destination in a minimal amount of time. All other kids thought that running a straight path was the best strategy. Only you recognized that a straight path might not be the best."

"I barely remembered that event. I am not sure if I had the insight of least- time principle on that day. It might be simply luck and I did that inadvertently," he said, smiling faintly but with a sense of proud.

Sitting down on a chair at the left side of his bed, I said, "Brother, I thought you were out of Hong Kong and drove trucks in Shenzhen and its nearby areas. Anyway, don't worry about other things. Take good rest and relax. Health is the most precious in life."

Calming down, he said, "Actually, I am in Hong Kong almost every day. A few weeks ago, I took a few days off to look for jobs. I just did not want you and Mom to worry too much about me. So I told her that I was away."

I said, "But you did not come home in the past few weeks."

He said, "Fore, I have to tell you the truth. A couple months ago, the business in the PC shop began to deteriorate. Last month's income could barely cover the rent and miscellaneous expenses. I therefore accepted an offer to drive trucks a few weeks ago to supplement the income. My task is to transfer goods between Hong Kong and China. The company provides a place for employees to stay overnight across the border. I start loading goods from factories there at 6 am and take them to this side. My work is done by 2 pm. I work in the PC shop in the evenings and cross the border at night. Actually, I made significant improvement in operating Linux systems in these two months. I know now how to setup a Linux network and connect it to the Internet. I might have worked too hard and got infected by this virus."

I said warmly, "Evans, your intention is good but your move is not.

Resign from the driving job and concentrate on the networking business. As your knowledge on networking has increased substantially, we can switch to doing business on network services. Starting from next week, you can come to Delight Inc. to help me maintain their network especially when I leave Hong Kong. To reduce the operating cost, we can close the shop. We can look for contracts to do network administration and maintenance. All we need is a cell phone."

I then taught him what I learned from Nun Anonymous about life. He felt more peaceful. After he had recovered from the virus, he came to work in Delight Inc. and concentrated on learning network administration.

After a few more months' training, he was able to set up and configure some basic Linux services, build a firewall or a proxy server, construct name and samba servers, administrate network file systems and database engines. He was able to write simple shell scripts and web pages. Each day he learned a little bit new. Little by little, pride piled over him. No longer was he a Windows-only administrator, no longer was it necessary for him to rely on GUI interface to carry out tasks.

At the time, I received a letter from Eric's manager, informing us that we had won the bid to maintain their company's network. Evans was very excited about the news. After signing the contract, he single-handedly extended their network to include Linux machines.

By the time I left Hong Kong, he was able to get a couple more contracts on maintaining Linux-Windows networks. The contracts generated revenue, which was big enough to pay his salary. It was almost incredible, and yet it was so. He suddenly found himself emerged from a demonic labyrinth. He again saw the world bright and joyful before him and no longer succumbed to suffocating fear of being jobless. Since then he enjoyed his new career more than anything he did before.

A few weeks before I left Hong Kong for America, one morning when I got to work at Delight Inc., Evans reported that the company's web server, which also consisted of a database engine had crashed and the data could not be recovered. I was not too surprise to learn that. The company was always in a rush, rushing to finish projects, rushing to get more business all the time. No body paid any attention to consolidation. It turned out that an engineer always telnet into the server to write his scripts and did not make any backup copy. Originally, I had setup an automatic replicating mechanism that could duplicate the server's data to another machine. However, for some reasons the backup machine had been turned off for one year and I was not aware of that, as I had delegated the work to Evans and other engineers. The hard disk was dead to the level that even the BIOS could not recognize it. One year's data, and one year's effort were lost in a sudden.

A Budha Temple in Hong Kong

A Budha Temple of Mount Hiei

# Chapter 10    Dot-com Bubble

When the company's president came in, a supple, lively man, with slightly graying hair, and with prudent eyes, the engineer reported in detail the data loss incident to him. The president was maddened by the news. He lost temper and began to yell at the engineer and Evans. As he came to my office in the usual manner, he looked at me intently, trying to discover if I had a solution to the problem. As I was a consultant, a guest in the company, he did not yell at me but certainly he was not happy.

I defended myself: "President, I am not trying to embellish things for you, but neither do I want to disavow or disguise the fact that I made the effort, strove and struggled even when and where I was at fault. But whether or not my attempt to make the system reliable and secure was conceit on my part, the disaster occurred – the company was not disciplined enough to cover accidental events."

The president was exceedingly emotional, although quite obviously struggling to control himself, and seemed to be trying to unburden himself from the weariness which had piled up and been haunting him since he knew about the loss of the data.

He said sternly, "Fore, I am not blaming anyone. I badly need the data back. Do you have any idea how to recover them? It would be very helpful even if we could only recover part of them."

I suddenly remembered a story about how Buddha healed a heartbroken mother who lost her child. I said, "President, I could recover the data if you can somehow obtain the serial number of a Windows machine that has held a company's data for more than five years. The serial number will contain clues to data recovery. You may call your enterprise friends to help find out such a serial number."

Upon hearing what I said, the president gained new hope and was excited. He immediately went to his office. I could see through the office windows that he was making phone calls. I began to regret what I just said. In the story, Buddha told the mother that he could make the dead child alive if she could ask for a bean from a family. But the bean must be from a family, which had not lost any beloved one. The mother knocked on all the families in the village only to find that each family had someone died. She then understood that death was part of life and began to accept the death of her child and moved on with her life.

I had perceived for some time that, with the popularity of Windows in the region, every company somehow would have their systems crashed or infected by virus leading to data loss. I therefore adopted the spirit of the story and hoped the president could inspire and calm down. But what if he had a friend who never lost data in the past five years? It would be very embarrassing for me to explain to him that I lied and I actually could not recover the data. Now I could only wish that if such a friend existed, he would not be the first one receiving the call.

Again, the world always goes against your will. After making one phone call, the president looked relaxed and put down the phone. He rose from his chair and walked slowly towards my office.

I took a deep breath, pretending that I was calm and at peace with the environment.

When he came in, I asked, "How many friends have you called?"

"One, " said the president, sitting on a chair.

"Did he lose any data in the past five years?" I asked, feeling uneasy and nervous.

The president was looking at me earnestly. He shook his head and smiled faintly. "He did not lose any data in ten years," said the president.

My heart was sinking. I was searching again, urgently searching for an excuse or explanation. I lost my words and did not know what to say.

"I must admit," said the president, still smiling, "that you have handled the incident admirably, most admirably."

He paused for a moment and looked at me, uncertain as to whether I was upset at him or not. My eyes caught his and found in them an expression of attention and friendliness, which eased me.

"Fore, I am stupid but not that stupid. I was kidding with you, " said the president. "Yes, my friend, a professional accountant running a small accounting firm had not lost any computer data in ten years. Then last year, his system crashed and lost all the data they entered in ten years. There was no backup. They had to reenter the data manually again. Since then they spent a lot more effort to protect the data. After hearing what he said, I immediately understood your intention. It is a blessing that we lose the data at this point, not ten years later. I apologize for my bad temper this morning."

He thanked me, and thereupon devoted a lot more care and resources to data protection and recovery.

Some years later when I revealed this incident, I was convinced that the president had not really made any relevant phone call. He just made up a story as I did to let me exit. He was the person who really possessed wisdom.

As flowers flourished and withered, as snow fell in Big Bear Mountain and melted, as dot-coms boomed and busted, two years had past. I came back to the US in 2002 Fall. Because of my absence in the US, almost all of my web-hosting clients had left; only a few friends remained. I had lost most of my starting capital as my company's communication equipment became junk. I came a full circle and got back to the starting point. When I started my Internet business I was in my early forties and now I was in my late forties. I had aged significantly and suddenly had a lot of white hair. I had traveled a path, which was at best in spiral if not in circle. But whichever way it went, I had to move on. Once more I was at the crucial point to make a decision. I was running out of time.

In two years, the high tech world had completely changed course. When the economy was booming, people could afford to do superfluous and foolish things, but when well-being gave way to affliction, life began to educate us. Throughout the booming years, dot-com startups recruited with unrealistic high salaries, held large parties, and advertised in Super Bowl tournaments. When accused of overspending, they pointed to the get-large- first essentials. In response to critics of their insanity, they claimed that innovations came from bold trials. And so on.

The days of affliction had come. Financial scandals of corporations sprang up here and there. The scandals led to the bankruptcies of many companies, which brought along with them jobs. Everywhere high tech jobs were lost, everywhere the dot-com boom faded, and no one saw any light. A great deal of fortune evaporated overnight. Silicon Valley was bleeding; millionaires became homeless. I had friends used to make $120,000 to $150,000 a year and now they had been jobless for over a year and a large portion of their previous income had been taxed. I had friends worrying about losing their jobs so much that each day they were panic when they went to work. So my condition was not the worst. At least I still had a job. Actually I was not poor. Besides the regular job, I had income generated from here and there ranging from consulting tasks to rental properties. And I gained knowledge, which was very important. I was a lot more proficient in Web programming and system configurations and I could do consulting work for any Internet related company; I had added value to myself. But still I felt bad that I failed my mission.

*Life is suffering.* Buddha had taught us. The dot-com madness proved Buddha's wisdom. There was ample evidence of Buddha's truth. *Suffering is caused by the wish for nonpermanent things and suffering ends when non- lasting things are rejected. The moment we take it willingly upon ourselves instead of fleeing it, suffering ceases to be horrible; suffering becomes new strength.* These are other truths from Buddha. It was the wish for nonpermanent things that made my friends painful. They felt embarrassed to transfer their kids from private schools to public schools and to move from a big house to a small house or an apartment to cash out the equity that they had built up. The pressure from peers might be the greatest pressure of all, at least for new immigrants. In America, living in a small house or an apartment can be very comfortable and enjoyable as long as your residing area has fresh air for breathing. But most of us would rather panic than move.

It was like playing ping pong in a tournament. You always compete with your peers. Even though you know that many players in the world can easily beat you, you will be joyful when you beat your peers and temporarily feel depressed when beaten by them. I thought about my friend Mike who started an Internet business using Windows NT. Though he was younger, I learned a lot of the philosophy of life from him. He was always smart and brilliant. *Would he be in the same boat as me?* I called him and setup a time to have coffee at Starbuck near a beach.

When I saw him, I could tell that the market crash had left a mark on him. but he was eager to tell me that he survived the market crash. He was able to make a living from his business by working full time on it but he failed to expand it further. Anyway, you would celebrate if you were still in the game after the market crash. I told him my condition that almost all my efforts paid for the Internet was in vain; I was a little disappointed but I was glad that I still had the teaching job. I had known Mike as a renown thinker and would like to know his point of view of the Internet business outlook. Mike could always look through the glass. He could look beyond the present and see what ordinary people could not see. Sometimes I felt that it was a waste for him to work full time on the business and that he should stay in the field of science; he might have a chance of doing something very significant. I was also puzzled that in conducting his business he was not as successful as I expected or as his intellectual IQ would predict.

Gazing at the blue ocean, he took a sip of coffee. Mike liked to do things in special styles. Even the way he sipped coffee looked well-rehearsed. He grabbed the cup with his left hand; moved it slowly towards his mouth and at the same time his right hand began to rise; he took a sip and simultaneously passed the cup to his right hand, which carried it back to the original position. The cup traveled an elliptical path each time he sipped and I noticed that his hands were actually making a classic Tai Chi elliptical movement. No one would notice this subtle special movement unless he watched it intentionally.

Putting down the cup, Mike pointed to the ocean and said, "Our current condition is like swimming to get on shore in a receding tide and wave. The shore is within an armful distance and is so near that you think you can reach it in a breath and a stroke. But right after you've made your stroke, the receding tide pulls you back for a distance you just have advanced and you are still at an armful distance from the shore. You struggle again and again but you are always just shy of your destination."

He paused, had another sip of coffee and continued, "Instead of struggling against the tide and wave, you could save your energy and let it take you to wherever it goes. It may take you to the remote water, far away from the shore; when you are tired of nothing moved, submerged and covered with fear, and at the point of giving it all up, the tide reverses and a big wave sends you to your destination in a single push. But humans are emotional beings. Emotion trumps reality. For the majority of us, we would rather struggle against the tide than let the tide carry us. The fear of not getting on shore has made us our own prisoners. Who would have the courage and wisdom to foresee that leaving is the foundation of arriving?" He sighed, and gazed at the distant ocean.

Mike was as sharp and intelligent as before and was cheerful and undefeated. But I felt that his confidence had actually faded a little.

I asked, "Did you ever foresee the bust of the dot-com? Would you start your Internet business if you have to do it again? " Mike did not answer my questions but stared at a plastic flower placed on the table. After a while, he pointed at the artificial flower and said, "Do you think that this flower is beautiful?"

I did not know why he suddenly brought up this question but I was certain that he wanted to make a point in answering my questions. I said, "It looks beautiful but I prefer a real one."

"Why do you think that a real flower is more beautiful than a fake one?" said Mike, smiling.

That was an interesting question that I never thought of. In general, I would say, "Because the fake one is not real" but then I had not answered the question. I thought for a while and said, "Maybe it lacks the fragrance."

Mike said, "Do you think that if you add fragrance to this artificial flower, you would like it as much as a real flower?"

I said, "I don't know but intuitively I would say I still like the real flower more. Honestly, I don't know why I like real flowers more."

"There are few who know, " said Mike, smiling again and gazing at the distant ocean. "Its because a real flower withers and dies."

That was something I never thought of neither. I said, "You mean it is the death of it that makes it beautiful?"

Mike nodded and said, "Yes. Things are beautiful only if they could change and perish. It is the fragility of life that makes life beautiful. It is the bust of dot-com that makes dot-com significant. Change is the way of nature. Immortals do not exist. There are a few who want to seek eternal life. They will be in vain. If the heaven would have passion, it would be aging. A single life will lose its meaning and value if it exists forever. The less time you have, the more valuable your time is."

I said, "So you mean dot-com boom and bust is a natural propencity and there's nothing to be afraid of."

He nodded again. Hesitated for a while, Mike pulled a card from his pocket and showed it to me. I recognized that it was a Tai-chi symbol.

Mike said, "This Tai-chi symbol, having two colors, Yin or black and Yang or white, or darkness and light, contains the world's wisdom. When the black grows to the extreme, the white begins to appear and eventually the white takes over and when the white grows to the extreme, the black begins to appear and the cycle repeats. Every sin already carries grace within it and vice versa. The whole universe is governed by this law."

Mike paused for a moment and continued: "I believe that the Internet will reboot in the not too distant future. When it reboots, there will be more opportunities than you can ever imagine."

I did not want to challenge his view. I did not agree nor did I disagree. Mike had another appointment and was leaving. I said good-bye to him and wished him good luck. After Mike had left, I looked into the blue ocean and watched the sun setting. The gentle warmth of the sun still lingered on the land. I was not sad nor was I happy. Mike's opinions left me in deep thinking. What was I seeking for all these years? Had I traded something eternal for the transitory?

I recalled that some years ago, the young beautiful Shalina came from Hong Kong to America to study. She was healthy, intelligent and passionate. Her smile was as sweet and pure as that of a new-born baby. She was always pleasant and treated others nicely. Unfortunately, her nice pleasant manner created a storm in the community of foreign students, which was dominated by male students in her university. She finished her study in four years and went back to Hong Kong to work in a TV station. After one year, she had become famous but at the peak of her fame, she resigned to become a nun in a temple. She had found peace and chose to serve Buddha. The temple was only a few miles from her home. Why did she bother to come to America, which was thousands of miles away and ended up serving in a temple nearby her home? And she didn't come here to study religion; she came here to learn a professional skill. But without going through this long journey, could she ever find her destiny?

Was it that the fragility of life had made life beautiful? Had God made us to become a fool in order to gain wisdom and we had to suffer failures in order to succeed? If Mike were correct, then everything existed in this universe had its position – death as well as life, sin as well as holiness, failure as well as success. If one could see through this, there was nothing deserving celebration when one gained and nothing deserving depressing when one lost. The only thing crucial was the participation as the fisherman once inspired me.

In that evening, I called Avogawa who co-founded Happy Web with me and had just come back from overseas. It turned out that we had a long discussion on Happy Web. Running Happy Web was an interesting experience to me. Once it was setup, the system worked 24 hours a day. If a customer subscribed the service, her credit card would be charged a fee, which would be deposited into our company's bank account. Everything was done by software and was automatic.

This experience inspired me to purchase some Amazon.com stocks. The company has a similar situation that when the system is setup, it works 24 hours a day to generate revenue. Of course, it's not exactly the same as ours since Amazon requires manpower to transfer the goods. Many people consider that Amazon is a retail company but one could also argue that it's a software company. It sells its software through the form of service of transferring goods. Its edge and success hinge on its software, not the sources or prices of its goods. Web programming is fairly simple and straightforward if the web site is set up to serve only a few customers. But if tens of millions of users visit your site each day, the task of building the site becomes very complex.

Wild Weird Shenzhen

# Chapter 11    Chimerical Rule

Situated on a hillside, full of evergreen woods and pockets of rich pasture where fine cattle grazed, was a ping pong playground converted from a warehouse. Its ceiling was composed of translucent glass windows that diffused and scattered sunlight to give players a feeling of brightness and softness. This was the table tennis club that I newly joined. Because of my loss in compassion in teaching, I decided while I was in the club I was not to regard myself as a teacher but solely as a businessman dealing with computer software and hardware. This attitude helped me get acquainted with other players more easily. The politeness and courtesy with which I was received in the club went a little beyond my expectation. I was granted full permission to use all the facilities and the privilege to challenge any player. I loved the expanse and spaciousness of this old hall, in which about a dozen ping pong tables were placed, each being surrounded by bluish green partitions with enough space for any playing style. I enjoyed the cleanness and simple comfort of the playing area, and on the very first day of playing, I was strongly attracted by the high quality and beauty of the tables. The players did not seem to be particular thankful to such a nice playing environment. Not only days but weeks passed before anyone brought up the discussion of the facilities. By then, I learned that the tables and the restructuring of the warehouse to form a ping pong playground were all sponsored by a club member called Rich Fan.

Some players explained to me that Rich Fan was a player's nickname; he was relatively rich and was a fan of table tennis. So everyone called him Rich Fan. With curiosity and intense interest, and with a certain degree of admiration as well, I longed to meet Rich Fan.

One day in the late autumn, I met a player called Owen who had joined the club for four or five years. I felt that I met him somewhere before but I could not recall where and when we met. His belly and his height made him look big. He had a thick beard but was semi-bald. He told me that he was an electrical engineer working in a local company that had just gone public a couple years ago. He had nice manners and was eager to help others but his temper was just as bad as his arrogant speech. I speculated that he might be Rich Fan whom others were talking about and most likely he had become rich because of his stock options. Though I was curious, I never asked him if he was Rich Fan as I always respected others' privacy. His game was significantly stronger than mine. However, I had learned the winning tricks from the Hong Kong trader and I sometimes managed to beat him by a small margin.

This drove him crazy and he was addicted to challenging me.

After two months of playing, Owen anticipated all my tricks and began to beat me most of the time. He eventually lost interest in playing with me. Then one day, I used my last tricks to beat him by a very small margin. He lost his temper and threw his paddle on the table. He repeatedly scolded himself stupid. Somehow, his behavior looked so familiar to me that I had a strong feeling I played him some years ago but I just could not recall the event. At this time, a tall thin player with a thick beard came to challenge Owen. I had never seen the player before. He smiled warmly and nodded to me; I felt that his gait was peaceful and his eyes humble. I nodded to signal them to go ahead to start the game.

I stood back and watched. Both of them were hand-shake players. The new player basically had no chance to smash the ball because Owen smashed and looped so frequently that his opponent was consumed in making blocks and returns. The concept of combat had been thousands of years old. If your attack is powerful enough, you do not need any defense.

As expected, Owen beat his opponent and introduced him to me.

He said, "This is Rich Fan whom people were talking about. He's from Carolina."

I shook hands with him, nodded, and stood at the side of a table. I saw his light-blue eyes and had a strange feeling. The gaze of his eyes might have been cold, but they were cheerful as well as penetrating, neither laughing nor smiling, but filled with a calm, quietly radiant confidence.

I jokingly said, "Nice meeting you. I thought you were from Hong Kong as Fan is a popular last name there but obviously, you are not."

Owen laughed and said, "No. He is rich and generous. He is a fan of table tennis. So every body here calls him Rich Fan."

Smiling and swaying his head, Rich Fan said, "No, not in that way. My first name is Richard and I am a ping pong fan. So they call me Rich Fan. Just call me Rich."

I didn't know why I liked him more than I liked Owen. Might be because of his modest appearance. By this time, I really wanted to learn the art of conducting a business and the secret of getting rich. I tried to get close to Rich Fan, sometimes acting like a sycophant, hoping to learn the art and the secret from him. I started by teaching him some winning tricks of the ping pong game that I learned from the trader. I explained the spirit behind the game, the importance of the integration of mind and body. The body nourishes the mind and the mind controls the body, I explained. I concluded the exposition with a demonstration of a push that the trader taught me. By relaxing and coordinating the hip, the waist, the hand and all parts of the body, one could generate tremendous power in a small movement to snap the ball with unexpectedly high speed. Rich later told me that he was greatly moved by the demo. It seemed to him that he was exposed to the game for the first time in his life. Behind the game being shown in his presence he sensed the world of Mind, the power of mind-body unification and the joy-giving harmony of control and freedom. He saw in those moments his emotions and the environment guided, and ordered by the spirit of the game, and when the demo ended, he had an emotion growing from within, not knowing whether to cheer or weep because it was over. I was sure he had exaggerated his feeling but no doubt I had given him an impressive introduction. At the end of the first ping pong lesson, I said to him in a friendly voice, "In no way is it easier for two men to become friends than in playing this game. It is a beautiful thing, and I hope that you and I will remain friends, Rich. Perhaps you too will teach me how to play your game." He shook hands with me, and made towards the hall exit; but just as he was about to leave, he turned round and said farewell with a look and a polite little inclination of his head.

Since then we met frequently and Rich learned the game with great interest. I patiently taught him all the techniques, along with the mind-body philosophy behind them. I hoped he would do the reciprocal. One day, I felt that the time was ripe and I began to test the water. I asked Rich Fan what one had to do to become rich.

"Could you tell us the rules of getting rich?" I asked, spinning a ball on the table.

Rich said with assurance, "Actually, there's only one rule."

I was amazed. I said excitedly, "One rule only? What's this golden rule?"

Rich looked earnestly into my eyes, nodded and smiled slightly, but did not say a word.

Disappointed, embarrassed, feeling something close to dismay, I said, "I didn't mean to ask about your business secret. I am a person of curiosity and simply want to learn everything that arouse my interest."

"You are anticipating," Rich said carefully. "Actually, I am not that rich and I feel embarrassed to tell you the golden rule."

I knew that everyone had his own secrets and its particularly true in the business world. It was certainly not appropriate for me to push for the answer. Though Rich did not tell me the golden rule, he did recommend me to read some books on investment and self-improvement. He told me that possessing technical talent was not enough to become rich; to be successful in business, one had to learn some more skills like marketing and communications. I took his words and began to read his recommended books that I never bothered to touch before. Eventually, I found that the books were helpful to my further investments.

I was patient and was not discouraged. I believed that Rich one day would teach me the tricks of getting rich like the way I taught him the tricks of winning the ping pong game. Little by little, I taught Rich more and more about the game. Each time I explained the game, he listened to me with unflagging attentiveness, refraining from the slightest interruption or question. He appreciated my teaching very much and after another two months, he began to beat me consistently.

It seemed that my long, mute courtship slowly softened his heart. I waited until one day Owen was with us. Before raising the issue of the golden rule of getting rich, I purposely asked Rich why he was so eager to improve his game. He then told us a secret. He wanted to beat a player who beat him before. We were surprised to learn that because we all knew that there were many players who could beat us easily. One might feel slightly depressed or disappointed at the moment of losing a match but he would forget it very soon and no one would keep the loss in mind. He told us that the player was in his twenties and had a very fast reflex. Rich showed slight emotions in his speech. He said, "The guy had no soul and I hate his attitudes. But he has solid defense. When I played him, I felt like hitting the balls against a wall; all of them bounced back to haunt me."

I said, "Time is on your side. When one ages, his reflex will get worse. Its easy to beat some one who only knows how to defend but not attack." I then promised to teach Rich the tricks of beating this kind of player. He thanked me gratefully.

At this point, instead of asking him the golden rule of getting rich, I asked him the factors that lead to his success. Owen interrupted and said, "Rich has a Ph.D. degree in mathematics. It seems that all his moves are well calculated and optimized." Only by that time did I know that Rich had an advanced degree. Since then, I felt that he behaved a lot more like an academic professional than a businessman. He was humble, full of confidence and nice to others.

Reluctantly, Rich said, "It has nothing to do with my advanced degree. Firstly, its my faith in God that contributes to my success."

He suddenly sighed and said, "Life is fragile!"

He paused and there was quietness among us. After a while, Rich continued: "Five years ago, the next day after I was narrowly beaten by the disgusted opponent, the one whom I mentioned to you that I wanted to beat badly, I had a serious car accident. I stopped my car in front of a red light and I saw from the rear mirror that a red car was approaching at full speed. All I could do at the moment was to hold the steering wheel tight. The red car crashed into the back of my car and I felt the shock but I was fine at that moment. A few days later, I felt a pain on my lower back and was diagnosed to find a dislocated joint at my back. Later, the pain was getting worse and I had no choice but to have a surgery. It took me three years to rehabilitate and now I still have to be careful not to hurt it again. Ironically, the accident made me think more about life and later I became a Christian. The accident was a time of tribulation for me but thank God I bore it bravely."

I tried to console him, quoting what Mike told me before, "The fragility of life makes life beautiful. Though you lost something and suffered pain in the accident, you gained wisdom and had become a better person. Every event has its value and position in this world."

"I devised the Golden rule of success when I lied up in the hospital, " said Rich, looking around with a warm smile. "Lets take a seat and I'll continue my story."

Rich seemed to open up and was suddenly eager to tell us his adventures. Owen, Rich and I took a bench and sat down. Rich put his paddle and an empty water bottle back to his bag.

He said, "In Africa and Thailand, elephants are friendly and kind. They move often but won't hurt any human. One day, a man saw a large group of elephants walking along the street of a town. He then got to the front and marched together with them. Many people in the town thought that he had magic power and could lead such a large group of elephants marching forward. Many rich people nowadays think that they are leading the world but in reality the world moves by itself. Its not led by any body. There may be a few exceptions but ultra rich people are just as bore as you and I."

I did not understand why he brought this up but I listened intently. Rich continued: "As I just mentioned, the glory of my success belongs to God. Without his help, I could not achieve what I have today. Ironically, I wouldn't believe in God if it were not because of the car accident."

Owen said, "You mean that religion is the most important factor contributing to your getting rich?"

Rich nodded.

As I was a Buddhist who can practice the religion with or without a

God, I raised the question, "Do you believe in the existence of God?"

"Yes, I do."

"Do you really believe that God exists and governs all our behaviors?"

Taking a breath, he said, "You have asked a wrong question. We communicate in words but unfortunately the word 'God' is not well defined. What you have in mind about the word 'God' could be different from what I have. Anyway, words are not good for conveying concepts; everything instantly becomes a bit different when we utter it. Arguing the existence of God will trap us within the maze of meanings, within the conflict of words."

He paused. With a warm smile, Rich pulled out from his bag the empty water bottle and a box of waxed dental floss. He cut away about two feet of floss and tied one end to the neck of the bottle. He passed the string to me and asked me to swing it. I swung it gently in the air and felt a force pulling my hand.

Rich said, "Do you feel the pull in your hand?"

"Yes."

"Why?"

"Because there is a centrifugal force acting on a rotating object, pulling it away from the rotating center."

"Does this centrifugal force exist? Is it really a force?"

"Yes and no. If you define 'force' strictly according to Newton's laws, it is not a force and it does not exist. However, we use this centrifugal force to model the physics of rotating objects and the model works well; the model simplifies calculations and explanations. So in this sense, you can say that it exists."

Smiling with radiant friendliness, Rich said, "You got the point."

Owen did not seem to agree. He challenged, "If something exists, it exists. If it doesn't, it doesn't. There's nothing to do with the model. The centrifugal force is not a physical force. It is something artificial that we simplify the explanation. In reality, it does not exist."

Rich asked lightly with again a smile that has open, childlike cordiality, "Is light composed of particles or waves?"

I said, "We can say it either way, depending on what model we are using. Sometimes, it's easier to use the particle model to explain certain phenomena while the wave model serves better in other times."

"The crucial point here is not to question the existence of God but to ask if the Satan-God model explains the world. From my experience and observations, I find that despite its simplicity, this model explains the world well and that's also why the model exists for so long and has been used by so many people. There could be some rare cases that the model breaks down, and we may need to modify or extend the model," said Rich, nodding.

I said, "I agree with Rich. You point your finger towards the moon to show your kid its beauty. If your kid just stares at your finger, she will then miss all the glory of the moon. Your finger is the tool, not the destination. The causality model in Buddhism explains a lot of phenomena but it does break down in some cases. We still can apply the model where it works just like the case that we apply Newton's model to construct the macroscopic world despite its complete failure in the microscopic world."

Owen argued, "If God really exists, why does so much unfairness, so much suffering occur? Why didn't he do anything?"

"You are tiring yourself, Owen," Rich said softly, his voice full of touching friendliness and solicitude. "Yes, he did something. He created you and you care about the unfairness and the suffering."

"How about if I don't care?" said Owen, grinning.

Rich said, "If you don't care, you won't raise this question. This is the beauty of the model. Once you want to seek the answer, you have the answer already."

Owen said, "But without your explanation, I wouldn't know the answer."

Rich said, "Then it doesn't mean the model is wrong. It is that you have not understood the model well. Despite its simplicity, you have to spend years to master it. Otherwise, like applying Newton's three laws, you have to rely on experts in the field to make the interpretations for you."

I listened silently. Rich continued to say: "Let me elaborate with some examples. Many people used to think that based on Newton's laws, an object could not fly in the vacuum. It turned out that rockets could. Many physics graduates cannot answer correctly if a human can turn a few rounds on a totally frictionless surface. The contradiction between the theory and reality is not that Newton's laws are wrong. It is because people have misunderstood the laws or have misinterpreted them. The better you understand the laws, the better interpretations and explanations you can make of them."

Rich continued to say: "Without the religious belief, I would be seeking in the dark and I will be lost from time to time."

It seemed that something of Rich's convincing argument, something of his cheerful tone and calm conquered Owen who began to bend and tend to agree with him. Owen said, "So your religious belief is the most crucial ingredient in your success in the spiritual sense."

"It is beyond the spiritual sense. The Bible contains all the general guidelines for conducting a business. All I have to do is to max out what God has made in me," Rich said, taking a breath.

Owen said, "Could you elaborate?"

Rich answered gracefully, "Certainly! Here are the few principles that I learn from Bible.

First, I need to be focus.

'An intelligent person aims at wise actions, but a fool starts off in many directions.' – PROVERBS 17:24 (GN)

I started out by doing one and only one thing in my business and added a few more features after I had established a solid base.

Second, I need to assume responsibility for my life.

'Each person must be responsible for himself.' – Galatians 6:5 (NCV)

'The lazy man is full of excuses..' – Proverbs 22:13 ( LB )

'In other words, integrity is a crucial ingredient in conducting my business. I must try my best to fulfill what I promise. A business would have no soul if its owner lacks integrity. Lacking integrity, a leader leads his country to chaos and moral decline.

Third, I must believe in myself.

'There is nothing I cannot master with the help of Christ who gives me strength.' – Phillippians 4:13 (LB)

Self-doubt is always the biggest enemy of conducting any business. Everyone has great potentials and God created everyone to be successful.

Fourth, I define my goals precisely.

'We can choose the sounds we want to listen to; we can choose the taste in food, and we should choose to follow what is right. But first of all we must define what is good.' – Job 34:3-4 (LB)

'Everything is permissible – but not everything is beneficial.' – 1 Corinthians 10:23 (NIV)

I have to clarify what I really want and I move in that direction without any regret. I would not regret my approach even if I failed because that's what I chose and that would be my destiny. And we have to recognize that not everything is beneficial. If you gain the world but lose your soul, you are still losing.

Fifth, I don't wait to begin.

'If you wait for perfect conditions, you will never get anything done.' – Ecclessiastes 11:4 ( LB )

'Tomorrow' is another worst enemy. How many dreams and hopes have been destroyed by the word 'tomorrow'? If I want to do something, I do it now, not tomorrow."

"I agree with your general principles. I am surprised that you can recite so many psalms precisely off your head," said Owen, showing a sign of admiration.

Rich said, "Because they are part of me. The words become flesh. I succeed or fail with them."

Owen said, "Did you ask God to bless your business in your prayers?"

"No, in my prayers, I never ask God for anything concerning my business," said Rich, shaking his head. "He has given us abundance already. I accept the world as is and thank God for what I have. Some people ask help from God even when they have a plumbing problem. To me, that's ridiculous!"

I said, "Actually, you can find similar principles in Buddha's teaching. Many people misunderstand that Buddhism concentrates only on asking humans to renounce themselves and to help others. But Buddha teaches us that in order to help others we must first help ourselves; we must first take good care of ourselves before minding others' business. The moment you see how important it is to love yourself, you will stop making others suffer."

"If a religious model does not explain and help solve social problems, it will vanish soon," said Rich, nodding his head. "I have one more point to add. Information exchange is the foundation of life. Consider a hypothetical event. A stone on Planet Mars fell into an abyss. Did this event ever happen?"

I said, "If somehow this information could be conveyed to a human, the event happened. Otherwise, it did not happen."

"Yes, we have consciousness and feel our existence because there is information exchange between us and the environment. Once the information flow to a life has been stopped, the life comes to an end, " said Rich.

I said, "So our body including our brain is just a tool for information exchange. What really makes us exist is the information flow."

Nodding, Rich said, "Yes. In principle, we do not need a body to support a 'Self'. Advanced 'humans' can exist in the Universe without bodies. They exist as long as there's information exchange among them. Of course, we are far from that advanced stage. But after billions of years of evolution, the stage 'humans without bodies' may be reached. God wants to ensure information exchange. Evil wants information exchange terminated. I believe in God though many people nowadays believe in Evil and think that information exchange is a cancer. God will triumph at the end."

Rich continued, "Everyone has her own way for improvement; you may play piano, go fishing or practice Yoga. In this modern world, there may be thousands of ways to enhance the utilization of your inner potential. My secret is to keep myself in good health, which is achieved by playing table tennis. I try my best to improve my game and to win tournaments but I do not play this game for the sake of playing. My ultimate goal is to have good health, which will lead to happiness and success."

Interrupting, Owen said, "So the game and tournaments are just tools for you to acquire health and happiness."

Nodding, Rich said, "Sure. I think this is the best sport for anyone who uses computers intensely. I cannot think of any other sports that can relax your eyes as much as this game does. When the ball bounces rapidly between you and your opponent, your eyes adjust the focus accordingly to follow the ball. This leads to rapid compression and relaxation of your eye muscles resulting in an excellent massage of them. Besides, when I smash a ball, my anger transfers from my body to the ball. On a bad day, I feel so much better after an hour of battling my opponent; all my anger is dispelled into the ball. I used to jog but jogging does not dispel anger. When I jogged and thought about something angry, the anger lingered around."

Now I also understood why my back pain syndrome went away after I resumed playing table tennis. The game could dispel my anger and my stress.

"Now can you tell us the golden rule of getting rich?" I interrupted.

"Yes, actually, I thought over this for a few years and I finally devised the golden rule but my rule may disappoint you."

Both Owen and I listened intently.

Rich spoke firmly, "The golden rule of getting rich is that there is no rule."

*What? There's no rule?* I was almost shocked. Isn't Rich making fun of us all the time? Obviously, he is not. He speaks seriously. I thought.

Rich paused and continued to say: "You cannot obtain salvation through teaching. You have to seek your own path. You have to stumble through much dirt and haunting before you can reach your destination if the destination ever exists. And there's no one who will guide you. Your only guide is your compassion. Actually, I tend to believe that becoming rich is just a random process. When Van Gogh was alive, his paintings did not worth anything and he lived in poverty. After his death, each of his paintings might worth millions of dollars."

Finally, I had learned the golden rule of getting rich. I was surprised but at least I learned that I had to find my own path.

Owen was just as amazed and asked, "Rich, what actually do you do in your business? Do you work full time in your business? How can you make so much money in three or four years?"

Rich replied, "I certainly can tell you about my business and I always hope more people can get rich via a path similar to mine. Currently, I work part-time in my business. Though I hold a Ph.D. degree in Mathematics, I teach in a high school. I love teaching. On the contrary, my wife works as an administrative staff in a University."

I could see that there's a sign of proud appearing in his face when Rich spoke about his business.

"I started the business a few years ago and I focused on hosting Web sites for others. I do not do any web page design for customers. I charged $9.95 a month for each domain and I maintain the same pricing scheme up to now. At the beginning, the hosting was simple. All I did was to provide a space for a company to store their web pages. As time goes along, to remain competitive, I've added more and more features to the hosting service; it is an evolution process. At the moment, for $9.95 a month, a customer can get many features such as audio-video streaming, online chatting and database support besides a huge storage space for web pages and e-mails.

My servers are Linux or BSD based and are clustered. All the software used is open-source and this is crucial for the survival of my company. Without the open-source, I could not survive the first wave of competitions. Actually, I would never bother to start the business if it were not because of the availability of free software; the risk would be too high to bear. A couple years ago, I added the service of domain registration for customers. I can tell you that last year my company has a revenue of about half a million dollars."

That aroused Owen's curiosity too. "Rich, I envied you very much. Let me tell you a secret," said Owen. "A few years ago, I too started a business on Internet but failed miserably; I closed it one year after I started it. Looking back, I felt that my ego was too big. I did not listen to advice and did not run the business properly. Anyway, do you have an office and many employees?"

His speech again reminded me of some one. Of whom? I could not make out. I stared at him and tried to figure if I had met him some years ago. However, I did not have time to make further analysis. I heard Rich answer proudly, "Basically, this is a one-man company. I write all the scripts, build and maintain the whole system. I have an office of a few hundred feet, which is used mainly to store the servers. I have only one part-time employee whose main job is to mail bills to clients. All the bills are generated from my scripts and basically everything is handled by computer programs."

I made a quick calculation on his financial status. As I was also in a similar business, I could estimate that his annual income could be well above half a million dollars. No wonder he was rich! I was also amazed by his productivity. He generated such a large annual income by working part- time. The crucial and significant point was that he did not achieve this by trading or speculating but by providing solid services to others. His success provided a model for the new economy. We do not have to pick up a job and work for a salary; an engineer or a scientist no longer has to work for a superior who may behave like a barbarian but knows nothing about technologies; they do not need to sell their souls any more. The realization of Einstein's ideal world of doing science has never been closer.

While I was examining the new model, Owen raised another question, "Why didn't you find a partner? Wouldn't that make your business foundation stronger and in a better position to expand?"

Smiling, Rich said, "I certainly prefer to work with partners if I could find some. The most important ingredient for a startup team to be successful is the integrity of the members. Ideally, you want to work with people with nice manners but it really doesn't matter much if your partners are rude or complain all the time as long as they do their job. However, if one member in the team lacks integrity, the whole business plan will be ruined even if he or she behaves very politely; your business is doomed to fail. A person who lacks integrity still can be your friend, or your wife but she simply cannot be your business partner. Unfortunately, it is difficult to know if a person has integrity until you work with him or her for a while. Certainly, a startup with three founders with integrity working together is always much better than one that has only one founder. The former will have a much better chance of succeeding. But if you are not sure if your potential partner has this quality, its better to work alone."

While I listened to Rich's theory on cooperation, I felt surrounded by the scholar's atmosphere. Vivid memories arose of my own ISP adventures, with the struggle and stress I endured in the early days along with other memories of the renewed intimate relations with Evans, the wound inflicted by the dot- com bubble burst and the healing by Nun

Anonymous. How well this courageous and knowledgeable scholar as well as entrepreneur contrived to fulfill his mission; how his wisdom and compassion had sheltered him from the dot-com crash; how circumscribed, concentrated and firm had the magic of his belief had guarded him from any harm. With a sigh, I tore away from this picture. I myself had gone another way, or rather been led, had been far more constrained and was beholden to go the path of pursuing quick wealth and not to compare it with the ways of others.

A California Beach

# Chapter 12    The Final Battle

It was late at night, cold and still. I sat in my room and tried to read but I could not. I looked through the windows and watched the cars in the distant freeway moving smoothly along. I looked lovingly into the stream of cars. A string of white pearls formed by the headlights moved in one direction while a stream of rear red lights moved in the other direction. I thought over the conversation with Rich. I envied and respected him. He achieved what Mike and I failed to achieve, so far. Might be Mike had taken a wrong approach. He tried to establish quick results by utilizing expensive commercial software applications of Windows. But the software cost had come back to haunt him and put a lot of constraint in his small company. Yes, Mike had gorgeous views of life and gorgeous philosophies of conducting a business. He might succeed one day too. But the American society was always cruel to losers. I observed a unique character of Rich. He was always confident in himself and he did not care about success or failures. Both Mike and I cared too much. We seemed destined to become victims of our own eagerness to succeed. We were too nervous about failures. Though the fisherman had inspired me to enjoy the process of participation, I still worried that people would look down upon me if I failed. I was curious why I was nervous all the time.

Before I came to America to study, a teacher told me that I might learn more about social science than my subject. He quoted someone's saying: "He who travels far will often see things far removed from what he believed was true."

After these years, I began to recognize the wisdom of his words. I looked back and examined the culture and environment in which I grew up. I was from a culture where both virtues and vice were abundant. One sad thing was that it had a long tradition of putting down individuals. Traditionally, people liked to glorify the emperors or leaders; without a great leader, a layman would live in dark abysses; if there's something significant achieved, its because of the emperor; one must sincerely thank the emperor and the elite group serving the emperor. The exact opposite happened in America. Individuals were more than willing to criticize the leaders and claimed credits for themselves. I observed that in America most parents tend to say positive things to their kids and have their kids believe that they are capable and have an abundance of talents. On the contrary, when I grew up in a small village, the parents tended to scold their kids with all negative descriptions that one could imagine: "You will never achieve anything...you

will certainly be a beggar ...you will become a prostitute...you will be
a sinner for a thousand years..." They were brought up in the same way
too. This certainly would have a very dampening effect on their kids'
development. I didn't know the current condition in Hong Kong but
I noticed that people were more innovative in scolding others: "You
are just like the Prime Minister of ...your IQ level is only better than
Tycoon L's son (who drops out of college and turns all profitable enter-
prises into money-losing businesses)..."

While I loved and respected all my teachers, I could not agree with
some of their teaching methods. I still remembered vividly how a primary school teacher used to scold some classmates who were physically strong but did not concentrate in class. I could feel that my classmates were hurt after the teacher scolded them. They were put down
by their parents at home and teachers at school. Eventually they lost all
their interest in study. To a lesser extent, I too suffered from this kind
of negative environment as I did poorly in primary school and was a
very average student in high school. I never had confidence in myself.
That induced a hard time in my life. The negative perceptions of myself had implanted deeply in my mind, which led to my nervousness of
handling things. Ironically, I became more confident in myself after I
started conducting Internet businesses though I encountered a sequence
of setbacks and failures.

Despite the frequent talks of 'American Arrogance', I noticed that
the public here was more interested in talking about American ugliness
than virtues. The willingness to talk about the ugliness might be the
ultimate strength of America. I remembered clearly more than twenty
years ago when I was in Hong Kong, I read the news of the Nobel
prize winners and found that every year, Americans dominated in the
field of Science and Medicine. Then there were always some American winners spoke out and warned, "It takes a long time for someone's
scientific work to get recognized. The prize reflects the excellent work
done many years ago. Given our current deteriorating education system, there's no way that Americans can dominate the prize in the future." At the time, I believed this was true. But twenty-five years had
past and Americans still dominated the prize. Yes, there are some draw-
backs in saying positive encouragements to the kids, but the benefits far
outweigh the defects. I was always curious about the small countries in
Northern Europe like Switzerland and Sweden. They only have a few
million citizens. Yet they could produce Science Nobel Prize Winners
and won the World Cups. Their national crime rates are particularly
low. I had never been to those countries but I speculated that they must

have a very peaceful and positive environment for kids to grow up so that everyone could utilize his or her potential to a greater extent. I once told the fisherman that I would not make further wishes but that night I made a wishful thinking.

*Parents shall not lift sticks against their kids. Neither shall they scold them anymore. They shall compose songs and bend their sticks to artwork. The world shall then flourish.*

I was not sure if I was dreaming or thinking but the wish had been a dreamer. What we learned best was to find excuses to justify our deeds, good or bad. What we desired and cared most was power. When our plant did not grow well, we did not blame the plant because we knew that we had done a poor job in growing the plant. When our kids went to school late often, we blamed our kids for not getting up early though we knew that the kids' living habit was shaped by us. That's the sad reality of humans. Like a drop of dew, like a flake of snow, pessimism precipitated in my mind, slowly, a little thicker every thought passed. I had been pessimistic for the past thirteen years. I was deep in memory. Then the phone rang and brought me back to reality.

Randalf, a friend from the table tennis club called. A player called Friedman wanted to challenge me next week and asked Randalf to make the arrangement. Without much thinking, I gracefully accepted the challenge. Randalf then explained that Friedman played me once and was narrowly defeated by me in Big Bear Club. That was five years ago. Since then he had been looking for me to ask for a rematch. Of course, he could not find me as I was out of this country for a couple years and had not played in Big Bear Club after my return. Friedman eventually met Randalf who incidentally knew me. He would come with Randalf to the club on that date. The ping pong world was so small. Since I beat him before, most likely, I could beat him again as I had learned a lot of tricks of winning the game from the Hong Kong trader. But I did not care much about win and loss. I was only curious why Friedman was so eager to challenge me. I tried to pull the clues together. With the information provided by Randalf, I searched in my mind the players I beat in Big Bear Club five years ago. It did not take me long to conclude that Friedman was Linux Fan.

Finally! He showed up again. It had been five years! I had been chasing him for years. I certainly wanted to see him, to settle the hacking of my system five years ago. I wanted to confirm that he failed in his business and that his attitude and ego didn't work. He should learn from the lessons and try to become a better person. We would settle all our hatred and disgust on the table. I grabbed three balls from a drawer and forcefully tossed them on my desk. The balls span rapidly on the desk to form a stable triangle. They span away my grief and anger before I went to bed.

I arrived at the club half an hour earlier than the actual appointment. Randalf was not there yet. I then saw Rich. I asked him to practice with me so that I could have some warm up. Rich was more than willing to do that. It turned out that he would also have a challenging match. He asked me to go through once the techniques I taught him. I patiently elaborated all the tricks I knew, explaining the importance of the movement, the timing difference between smashing and looping, the theories of attack and counter attack, and the mental attitude during a match. It took me almost half an hour to finish the coaching. I would feel happier to see him beating his opponent than myself winning my challenging match, as I owed him the teachings of running a successful business.

Right after we finished the workout, I saw Randalf and Owen walking into the hall from the other end. We waved to each other but they did not come over. Randalf looked at us for a while and then took a table and began practicing with Owen. It seemed that they were doing some warm up to prepare for a match. I looked at Owen again, watching his playing style carefully. I tried to pull things together and I recalled that Randalf said he would come together with Friedman. I seemed to have the whole picture.

So Owen was Linux Fan as I had long speculated. Owen Friedman! I now knew his full name. I felt the pressure released from me and breathed a sigh of relief. This time, almost for sure Owen would beat me in the challenging match, but for sure I knew that he failed miserably in his business. I was prepared to fight him but I did not care about the outcome anymore. Actually, he had lost. He fared much worse than I in his business. I still remembered clearly and vividly his arrogance, his big ego, his rudeness and his bad temper in the argument five years ago. He was a boor. He thought he knew all the answers and was on top of the world. The debate was like a scar cut in my heart though time had healed the wound. At the moment, I was joyful I won over my foe and I had the final laugh. I had waited this moment for a long time. What should I tell him when we met in a moment? I should praise his ping pong skill and then I would ask him about his business. I would like to see his embarrassing and blunt expression. A winning joyfulness crept into my mind and enveloped me. However, my joyful feeling was short-lived. I then felt sorry for both of Owen and myself. Both of us were losers. There was nothing to celebrate.

Wouldn't it be much better if both of us succeeded in our businesses? Actually, Owen had become my friend. Wouldn't it be better if I had a friend succeeded in his business though I failed in mine? The joyfulness turned into shamefulness. All I cared was that if people respected me, which in fact was an indication of lack of confidence. What I had ignored was that one's perception of the world being in and around us could change. I had concentrated on one side of a person but often had ignored the other side. I had only loved certain people who agreed with me, let me have my way, or provided me with advantages, while I had not loved, and might even hate, those whose thinking and feeling was different from my own, who opposed me or put obstacles in my way. And this had created the burden for me. How stupid had I been! My hard feeling towards Linux Fan suddenly dissolved and the invisible burden evaporated. I had been stupid to build up this burden. I had been stupid to shoulder the burden for five years. A higher-level joyful feeling resurfaced in my mind. I should have acquired this joyfulness five years ago. But like Shalina who took a round trip to America in order to settle in the service of a Buddha temple near her home, I too had to travel a full circle to shed the burden. I took a glance at Owen. He no longer looked arrogant to me. He no longer seemed alien. He too was a seeker and bore the common weakness of humans. He too had suffered from the temptation of Red Dust. A stream of thoughts flowed through my mind. When this joyful experience had repeated itself a few times, I found myself enveloped by a glorious feeling of happiness, thick and full, sweet and fresh, like a garden fragrance or sea breeze.

Noticing the joyful appearance in my face, Rich asked, "Why are you so happy suddenly?"

"Because I see you!" I said, " Rich, you looked a little nervous today? Is it because of the challenging match? Who is your opponent?"

"Yes. I still have no confidence to beat him!" answered Rich, forgetting to tell me the name of his opponent.

"Why are you so worried about the win and loss? You can beat many players including myself easily but still many people can beat you. You are a successful businessman and engineer. You are serious about whatever you do and pay great efforts to achieve supremacy. That is delightful, but this is a game. I imagine that you try to exalt this wonderful game into something akin to the way you run your ISP business. But the game remains a game and a game always has win and loss, victory and defeat."

"I know what you mean but I want to beat this guy badly. I lost to him once! He's disgusted."

"Why do you hate him so much?"

"The guy had no soul. I had a quarrel with him before. He was a keen propaganda for Evil Empire. Many people suffered from the evil behaviors of the Empire. Nothing could make me happier than beating a loyal Evil follower."

I felt a little uneasy about what Rich said but I tried to calm him.

"Rich, have you ever noticed that the forms I teach you to win are quite different from the way I play?"

"Yes, I had long noticed that and wanted to ask this question. I didn't ask only because I worried that the question might offend you," said Rich.

I smiled and said, "You wouldn't. You should have asked."

Rich said, "When I loop a ball, I do not let my paddle go beyond the level of my nose so that I can recover my position for the ball to come back. But you always follow the motion of the ball, swing your whole body and draw a full circle in the air with your paddle."

I said, "That's because I taught you the winning form. Your motions are optimized to win the game."

"Doesn't every body learn a style to win the game?" said Rich.

"No. My playing style is optimized for health. My motions are smoother and natural. This has a better effect for health but is slightly inferior to your playing style in winning a game. I know that you always want to win a match, so I only teach you the winning style," I explained.

Rich said, "You awaken me. After today's match, could you teach me the style that is optimized for health? I prefer health than winning matches."

I said, "But if you were to lose today's match in order to learn the healthy style, would you still prefer to do that?"

Rich began to hesitate. Before letting him say anything, I continued: "What's evil in your mind may not be evil in others' mind. That's the way we are made. I agree that evil in one's mind will grow when one gains power. Men desire power most. Almost nobody could escape this sad fate. All leaders with an extremely rare exceptions claimed to strive power for the sake of the good. But once they gained power, they all became obsessed and numbed by power and loved it for its own sake. Einstein was one of the few who could renounce power. He had found something more beautiful and the force was so powerful that it could overwhelm his desire for power."

"You have a point but Evil Empire has been creating too much suffering and injustice. I feel I have a mission to stop their evil deeds," said Rich, sighing.

"Buddha had taught us that every event in the world has its reasons. Life is suffering. Suffering has reasons. Suffering shapes characters. Great characters are not made of luxuries; they are shaped by suffering. Through the suffering, you are perfected to fight the evil. But I don't see how you can turn back Evil by beating one of its supporters in a game. Try to be open and free. Forget the win and loss. Enjoy the match."

Rich did not say anything but gazed at a distance. He seemed to think over what I just said. I took a few breaths and kept quiet. It seemed a long time had past and Rich seemed to be more relaxed.

I first broke the silence. I asked, "Has your opponent come yet?"

"I don't know. I had not seen him for a long time. Actually, Randalf made the arrangement of our match."

"Really? He arranged my match too."

"Yes, Randalf knows all the active players in the region."

Hearing what Rich said, I was more suspicious. I asked, "When does your match begin?"

"In about ten minutes."

"Oh, my dear! My match will also start in ten minutes too."

"When did you last play your opponent?"

"Five years ago."

"Where?"

"Big Bear Club!"

All these seemed to point to something. Was it fate or was it a consequence of my deeds? Gradually I gathered my thoughts again and mentally reviewed the entire path of the events, from the very first days I encountered Linux Fan. I was totally deceived and had thought Owen was Linux Fan. I had been subjective in observing the world and making conclusions. I almost wanted to laugh. Buddha had long taught us not to cling to any concept or doctrine. But not only had I clung to my imagination about Linux Fan, I also had tried to associate him with someone I did not like. I could not accept that he actually was my friend, my teacher and someone I envied and respected. If I had not clung to the misjudgment, I would have recognized Rich long time ago. Rich was the real Linux Fan, not Owen! I was sure about that now. Rich too had clung to the past and his imagination. He unconsciously refused to associate his imaginary foe with his friend who taught him how to beat his foe. We were seekers. We concentrated on the things we seek and saw nothing else. We both lost on our way of seeking.

Finally, I said, "So you never played him again since the match, Mr. Richard Friedman?"

"Yes. Excuse me. How do you know my last name?"

Calmly, I said, "Randalf told me that. Your opponent has arrived!"

Rich looked around and asked, "Where?"

"He is right in front of you!"

He gazed at me with surprise and asked, "What do you mean?"

"Mr. Richard Friedman, five years ago, in Big Bear Club, a Linux fan had a big argument with a Windows fan. You were the Linux fan and I was the Windows fan. You hate your opponent so much but you could not even recognize him when he is right in front of you."

Amazed, he gazed at me. Then he shook his head and said, "No. This could not be true. How old are you now?"

"I am in my late forties."

"That's what I thought too. The Windows fan I met was a lot younger. He was in his twenties. He may be in his early thirties now."

"Did he tell you his age?"

"No. But that's how he looked. He had very fast reflex action."

"Appearance is deceiving. I had fast reflex five years ago."

"He had thick dark hair but your head is full of white hair."

"Five years ago, I did not have a thread of white hair."

"He had a mustard and a beard."

"I used to have a mustard and a beard."

Shockingly, his voice was almost shriveling. "You are Windows Fan?"

"Certainly, five years ago, we played the 21 points game, the best of three. I beat you -3, 23, 19."

Coolly, attentively, we gazed at each other. For a while Linux Fan seemed lost in thought and crestfallen. Silently, he gazed out into the expanse of the quiet pasture. The autumn scenery and clear air composed a picture of peacefulness and harmony. Then he turned hesitantly and I saw his eyes return from the abstraction and focus on me. He received me with a friendly look, a slightly questioning, half-compassionate, half-amused look of amazement – such a look as a child might have for discovering a new toy. Slowly, he looked upward and threw the ball high up into the air. The ball dropped with a speed that if well-utilized could generate a non-returnable powerful serve. But at the moment the ball contacted his paddle, he made a backward jerk that absorbed the impact and struck it softly with an elliptical spin, his signature of friendly greeting. By this serve alone, this serve which contained a trace of benevolent compassion and the hint of a relationship that had come into being between us, the relationship between two foes – by this serve alone, Rich Fan challenged me to accept a new relationship, the one between friends, between masters and students. I turned my body. Slowly and softly, like a Tai Chi movement, I drew a smooth full circle in the air and returned the ball with a backhand flip that carried anti spin. It signified the start of a new relationship as well as love and concern and appreciation. By this exchange of serve and return, we banished any thought of revenge and hate in our heads. It bound us in discipline and service, in friendship and respect.

Since then Linux Fan and I became good friends. He taught me about the utilization of open-source software to conduct Internet businesses. That was the path to freedom. He claimed.

Table Tennis Game

Other books by the same author

# An Introduction to Video Compression in C/C++
by *Fore June*

March 2010
ISBN: 9781451522273

www.ingramcontent.com/pod-product-compliance
Lightning Source LLC
Chambersburg PA
CBHW071227050326
40689CB00011B/2483